W9-CHI-051

BISCOTTI

BISCOTTI

RECIPES FROM THE KITCHEN OF
THE AMERICAN ACADEMY IN ROME

BY MONA TALBOTT & MIRELLA MISENTI

FOREWORD BY ALICE WATERS

PHOTOGRAPHY ANNIE SCHLECHTER

ROME
SUSTAINABLE
FOOD
PROJECT

The Little Bookroom

New York

© 2011 The Little Bookroom
Text and recipes © 2010 Mona Talbott
Photographs (unless noted below) © 2010 Annie Schlechter
Book design: Annie Schlechter
Book production: Adam Hess

Library of Congress Cataloging-in-Publication Data

Talbott, Mona.
Biscotti : recipes from the kitchen of the American Academy in Rome :
Rome sustainable food project / by Mona Talbott and Mirella Misenti ;
foreword by Alice Waters ; photographs by Annie Schlechter.
p. cm.
Includes index.
ISBN 1-892145-89-8 (alk. paper)
1. Cookies. 2. Cookery, Italian. 3. American Academy in Rome.
4. Sustainable living. I. Misenti, Mirella. II. Title.
TX772.T37 2010
641.5945—dc22
2010008203

Photos pages 57, 91, 96, 108, 114 & 116 © 2010 Matthew Monteith

Printed in The United States of America

Published by The Little Bookroom
435 Hudson Street, 3rd floor
New York NY 10014
editorial@littlebookroom.com
www.littlebookroom.com

ISBN 978-1-892145-89-5

10 9 8 7 6 5 4 3 2

TABLE OF CONTENTS

FOREWORD

The recipes in this book are a perfect expression of the values of conviviality and purity embodied by the Rome Sustainable Food Project. Each of these cookies brings with it a taste of time and place—the ingredients are seasonal, organic and local—and no cookie is so big or so sweet that eating one will interrupt conversation at the end of a meal. In this way, the cookies are a delicious and beautiful expression of the American Academy's intention of inspiring discourse between scholars of many disciplines.

The Rome Sustainable Food Project is very close to my heart. When I first visited the American Academy in 2006, I was so impressed by its beauty I immediately wanted to contribute to a program that would make the food reflect its high ideals of scholarship and art. Food had to be a part of the experience for everyone who came, because I knew it was capable of binding the whole community together as nothing else could. Under the direction of Mona Talbott—a chef who is also an artist—the meals have exceeded my expectations and have become an indispensable element of life at the Academy.

Alice Waters
Berkeley, California
May 2010

ROME SUSTAINABLE FOOD PROJECT

At the Rome Sustainable Food Project, we think about *biscotti* the same way we think about all the food we prepare for the American Academy in Rome: thoughtfully and carefully. The ingredients are sustainable, mixing and baking is done with precision, and the final product is delicious, honest, and hopefully memorable.

Indulgent or nutritious, each *biscotti* is the essence of its main ingredients: hazelnut, chocolate, lemon, pistachio, or simply butter, flour and sugar. We decided early on that our *biscotti* would be *piccolini*—small—like a great Roman *espresso*; two or three bites would be enough to satisfy.

At noon each day a plate of freshly baked *biscotti* is placed on the end of the AAR bar to tempt the noisy crowd that drinks *espresso* after lunch. We know from experience that warm *cioccolata e nocciole* sell out quickly and that the handsome AAR gardeners are particularly fond of the *baci di cocco*. The library staff who come for coffee at precisely 3:30 love the *biscotti di fichi*; *bolle di neve* is relished by the friendly library reader from Bologna. It seems that everyone has a favorite.

The Library Tea is served Monday to Friday at 4:30 pm accompanied by a large plate of *biscotti*, which entices fellows and staff out of their studios and offices and into the Academy *salone* for a *piccolo pausa*, a small break, to talk with the Italian scholars who study in the AAR library. Once a week we feature *biscotti* with *tisana* at dinner, and for dessert we often serve *biscotti* alongside *gelato* or bowls of macerated fruit.

Biscotti are tucked into bag lunches, nestled into welcome baskets for AAR visitors, and packaged for sale in the Academy bar. They have become a delicious part of the daily life at the Academy, requests for recipes are frequent, and this encouraged us to write our first RSFP cookbook.

The Rome Sustainable Food Project launched in February 2007 after six months of tryouts and ingredient sourcing. It was seen as a bold move—American cooks cooking Italian food in Rome? *Ma dai!* We had enthusiastic support from the Academy management and

Fellows, but skepticism from the Italian staff. The food before had been dreadful, but it was familiar. Nervous yet determined, Chris Boswell and I jumped in, trusting that with exceptional ingredients, our Chez Panisse training, and years of experience, we could win over the Americans and Italians. We are proud to say we have been successful and the RSFP has forever transformed the culture of the American Academy in Rome.

When we began, the AAR kitchen was run down and the pastry department was a three-foot counter between the pot sink and the oven. (The kitchen has since had a major renovation.) I had a hard time keeping up with the demand for muffins, scones, cakes, and cookies, and it soon became obvious I would need to find a part-time pastry cook. Mirella Misenti was then our very curious and hardworking dishwasher. She had one eye on us at all times and spoke only Italian. Every Saturday she brought in a homemade apple cake for staff lunch. One week we asked her to make her cake using our organic ingredients. The difference was remarkable, and she had a culinary flashback: not only was it better tasting, it reminded her of the cakes her grandmother made in Sicily when she was a child.

Although Mirella had never worked as a professional cook, like many Italians, she grew up cooking alongside her mother, aunts, and grandmother. She had the passion, pride, and perfectionism one finds in great pastry cooks and was relieved to stop washing dishes when we needed her help.

When we reopened after our first summer break, I began translating American cookie recipes for Mirella, teaching her how to make big batches of peanut butter cookies, snickerdoodles, chocolate chunk cookies, coconut macaroons, and gingersnaps. All these recipes were foreign to her, but Mirella was eager to learn. She slowly began to make some of her favorite Sicilian *biscotti*, which was a revelation. Sicily has a rich history of confections and each little cookie is truly a *bella figura*. They were elegant and made the American cookies seem almost childish. It was an exciting moment when Italian *biscotti* took their rightful place at the AAR. Mirella and myself, along with contributions from many visiting cooks and interns, grew our *biscotti* repertoire to these fifty recipes. Without Mirella there would be no RSFP *Biscotti* book—she was the key ingredient.

The *biscotti* recipes are titled in Italian because we are primarily an Italian-speaking kitchen. They are divided into five categories—Milk and

Wine; Nuts; Honey, Citrus, and Spice; Meringue; and Chocolate—because we think of the recipes in this way.

The *biscotti* listed under the Milk and Wine category are mostly dry and not too sweet and are meant to be stored in your cupboard, ready to eat when you need them. Several are traditional Italian *biscotti* that are eaten for breakfast with *caffè latte* or dipped into a glass of *vino dolce*. To an American palate they can taste surprisingly plain but make complete sense when eaten as they were intended.

The *biscotti* in the section entitled Nuts are some of the best in the book. Lazio, the province in which Rome is located, cultivates incredible hazelnuts and walnuts that we use extensively in the RSFP kitchen. The majority of Mirella's Sicilian *biscotti* fit in this category. Delicious pine nuts, pistachios, and almonds are featured in these fourteen recipes.

The Honey, Citrus, and Spice section recalls Italian medieval and Renaissance kitchens and the influence of the spice trade. Many of these recipes came from our friends or were developed in our kitchen. The Academy has a large citrus grove and we are always seeking to use lemons and oranges in our cooking.

Meringue cookies are delicate and practical. In the RSFP kitchen we make a lot of fresh pasta and always have the leftover egg whites on hand, ready to use. Meringues keep well and are a great finishing touch for a fruit-based dessert.

The five recipes for chocolate *biscotti* are, to no one's surprise, the most popular with the AAR children. We have yet to secure a source for Italian organic chocolate chips so we chop up a large block of bittersweet chocolate for all these recipes, with great results.

The recipes have been scaled down for the home kitchen, but the recipes can be scaled back up for large-batch cooking in an institutional setting. The best way to have consistent quality is to weigh all your ingredients and we have provided you with gram measurements, which we find is the simplest and surest way to do this.

Buon lavoro!

Mona Talbott
Rome, May 2010

RECIPES

CANTUCCI DI PRATO
ALMOND CORNMEAL COOKIES

YIELDS 60 COOKIES

We keep cantucci di Prato, *based on a recipe in the incredible* Zuni Cafe Cookbook, *stocked in the bar at all times. Every region of Italy has a version of this kind of biscotti and this recipe is our standard.*

110 g / 4 oz raw almonds

175 g / 1¼ cups all-purpose flour

10 g / 2 tbsp fine cornmeal

2 g / ½ tsp baking powder

2 g / ½ tsp salt

2 g / ½ tsp anise seeds

60 g / ¼ cup + 1 tsp butter

138 g / ½ cup + 3 tbsp granulated sugar

1 large egg

10 ml / 2 tsp anise liqueur

Preheat the oven to 150ºC / 300ºF.

Spread the almonds evenly on a baking sheet and toast for 12–15 minutes. When the nuts have cooled, transfer them to a cutting board and chop coarsely.

Combine the flour, cornmeal, baking powder, salt and anise seeds in a medium-size mixing bowl.

Cream the butter and sugar at high speed until light and fluffy. Add the egg and mix until well incorporated. Change to low speed and add the liqueur. Add the dry ingredients to the butter mixture in two parts and then gently fold in the almonds until evenly combined. Wrap the dough in plastic film and refrigerate for 15 minutes.

To bake, preheat or reset the oven to 180ºC / 350ºF.

Remove the dough from the refrigerator and divide it in two. On a floured surface form each portion into logs 2.5 cm / 1 inch in diameter. Transfer the logs to a cookie sheet lined with parchment paper and bake for 20 minutes.

Once cool transfer the cookie logs to a cutting board and cut them into approximately 1-cm / ½-inch slices with a serrated knife. Lay cookies flat on cookie sheets lined with parchment paper and bake for 6–8 minutes, until golden brown.

These cookies will keep well in a sealed container for up to 1 month.

CANTUCCI DI NOCI E CANNELLA
WALNUT AND CINNAMON COOKIES

YIELDS 60 COOKIES

This variation of biscotti di Prato *is delicious as a part of a mixed cookie plate, which we often serve at the daily Library Tea.*

110 g / 4 oz walnuts

175 g / 1¼ cups all-purpose flour

10 g / 2 tbsp fine cornmeal

2 g / ½ tsp baking powder

2 g / ½ tsp salt

1 g / ¼ tsp black pepper

4 g / 2 tsp ground cinnamon

60 g / ¼ cup + 1 tsp butter

138 g / ½ cup + 3 tbsp granulated sugar

1 large egg

10 ml / 2 tsp Nocino, a green walnut liqueur

Preheat the oven to 150ºC / 300ºF.

Spread the walnuts evenly on a baking sheet and toast for 12–15 minutes. While the nuts are still warm, place them inside a clean tea towel. Gather the towel into a secure bundle and roll the nuts in a circular motion to loosen and remove some of the skins, and with them any extra bitterness. Lift the nuts out of towel, leaving behind the skins, and transfer to a cutting board. Coarsely chop the nuts by hand.

Combine the flour, cornmeal, baking powder, salt, pepper and cinnamon in a medium-size mixing bowl.

Cream the butter and sugar at high speed until light and fluffy. Add the egg and mix until well incorporated. Change to low speed and add the liqueur. Add the dry ingredients to the butter mixture in two parts and then gently fold in the walnuts until evenly combined. Wrap the dough in plastic film and refrigerate for 15 minutes.

To bake, preheat or reset the oven to 180ºC / 350ºF.

Remove the dough from the refrigerator and divide it in two. On a floured surface form each portion into logs 2.5 cm / 1 inch in diameter.

Transfer the logs to a cookie sheet lined with parchment paper and bake for 20 minutes.

Once cool transfer the cookie logs to a cutting board and cut them into approximately 1-cm / ½-inch slices with a serrated knife. Lay the cookies flat on cookie sheets lined with parchment paper and bake for 6–8 minutes, until golden brown.

These cookies will keep well in a sealed container for up to 1 month.

CANTUCCI DI PINOLI E ROSMARINO
PINE NUT AND ROSEMARY COOKIES

YIELDS 60 COOKIES

This is our third variation on the biscotti di Prato *cookie and maybe the favorite. Subtle yet herbaceous, they complement an after-dinner tisane.*

110 g / ¾ cup pine nuts	Preheat the oven to 150ºC / 300ºF.
175 g / 1¼ cups all-purpose flour	Spread the pine nuts evenly on a baking sheet and toast for 8–10 minutes or until golden.
10 g / 2 tbsp fine cornmeal	
2 g / ½ tsp baking powder	Combine the flour, cornmeal, baking powder, salt and rosemary in a medium-size mixing bowl.
2 g / ½ tsp salt	
4 g / 2 tsp rosemary, minced	Cream the butter, sugar and lemon zest at high speed until light and fluffy. Add the egg and mix until well incorporated. Change to low speed and add the Marsala. Add the dry ingredients to the butter mixture in two parts and then gently fold in the pine nuts until evenly combined. Wrap the dough in plastic film and refrigerate for 15 minutes.
60 g / ¼ cup + 1 tsp butter	
138 g / ½ cup + 3 tbsp granulated sugar	
Grated zest of 1 lemon	
1 large egg	
10 ml / 2 tsp Marsala	To bake, preheat or reset the oven to 180ºC / 350ºF.

Remove the dough from the refrigerator and divide it in two. On a floured surface form each portion into logs 2.5 cm / 1 inch in diameter. Transfer the logs to a cookie sheet lined with parchment paper and bake for 20 minutes.

Once cool transfer the cookie logs to a cutting board and cut them into approximately 1-cm / ½-inch slices with a serrated knife. Lay the cookies flat on cookie sheets lined with parchment paper and bake for 6–8 minutes, until golden brown.

These cookies will keep well in a sealed container for up to 1 month.

CIAMBELLINE ELENA
RING COOKIES WITH ANISE SEEDS

———

YIELDS APPROXIMATELY 70 COOKIES

AAR colleague Elena Tinaburri shared her ciambelle recipe with the RSFP and we think it's the best-tasting version in Rome. Ciambelle are traditionally served with Frascati wine from nearby Castelli Romani.

20 g / 3 tbsp anise seeds

150 ml / 5½ oz white wine

150 ml / 5½ oz olive oil

600 g / 4⅓ cups all-purpose flour

150 g / ¾ cup granulated sugar

Pinch of salt

9 g / 2¼ tsp baking powder

150 g / ¾ cup sugar, for coating

Soak the anise seeds in the white wine for 1 hour. Strain the seeds and reserve the wine for the cookie dough.

Whisk the white wine and olive oil together in a small bowl.

Combine the flour, sugar, salt, baking powder and anise seeds and mix gently by hand until a soft dough forms. On low speed, add the wine and olive oil and continue to mix until the dough forms a soft ball. Cover with plastic film and let it rest for 30 minutes at room temperature.

To bake, preheat the oven to 180ºC / 350ºF.

To shape the cookies, pinch small pieces of the dough and use your hands to roll each piece into a rope approximately 15 cm / 6½ inches long x .5 cm / ¼ inch wide. Pinch the ends of the ropes together to form a ring shape. The dough will shrink as it relaxes.

Gently press the face of each ring into the reserved granulated sugar. Transfer the cookies to sheet pans lined with parchment paper, leaving 2 cm / ¾ inch between each cookie.

Bake for 15–18 minutes, until golden brown.

CIAMBELLINE CON FARRO E MIELE

RING COOKIES WITH FARRO AND HONEY COOKIES

———

YIELDS 48 COOKIES

This is a breakfast cookie, lightly sweetened and made wholesome with the addition of farro flour.

185 g / 1½ cups farro flour

240 g / 2 cups all-purpose flour

12 g / 1 tbsp baking powder

215 g / 1 cup butter

100 g / ½ cup sugar

2 large eggs

80 ml / ⅓ cup honey

15 ml / 1 tbsp vanilla extract

35 g / ¼ cup raw sesame seeds

50 g / ¼ cup granulated sugar, for coating

Combine the farro flour, all-purpose flour and baking powder in a small bowl.

Beat the butter, sugar, eggs and honey and vanilla until smooth. Add the flour and mix until the dough comes together. Wrap the dough in plastic film and refrigerate for 30 minutes.

Preheat the oven to 180°C / 350°F.

To shape the cookies, pinch small pieces of the dough and use your hands to roll each piece into ropes approximately 15 cm / 6½ inches long x .5 cm / ¼ inch wide. Pinch the ends of the ropes together to form a ring shape.

Transfer the rings to cookie sheets lined with parchment paper spaced 2.5 cm / 1 inch apart. Sprinkle with sesame seeds and granulated sugar.

Bake for 10–12 minutes, until golden brown.

These cookies keep up to 1 week in a sealed container.

BISCOTTI REGINA

SESAME SEED COOKIES

───────

YIELDS 40 COOKIES

The recipe for these not-too-sweet sesame cookies originates in Arab-influenced Sicil-ian cuisine. We like to serve them with mint tea and candied citrus peel.

167 g / 1 cup + 3 tbsp all-purpose flour

58 g / ¼ cup + 2 tsp granulated sugar

3.5 g / ½ tsp baking soda

50 g / 3 tbsp + 2 tsp butter

20 ml / 1 tbsp + 1 tsp milk

1 egg yolk

2 g / ½ tsp grated lemon zest

50 g / ⅓ cup raw sesame seeds

Combine the flour, sugar and baking soda until the dry ingredients are well sifted. Add the butter, milk, egg yolk and lemon zest all at once to the dry mixture and mix slowly until a soft dough forms. Wrap the dough in plastic film and refrigerate for at least 30 minutes.

Remove the dough from the refrigerator and form it into 40 (7 g / ¼ oz) balls. Transfer the sesame seeds to a small mixing bowl and gently press the seeds into each ball as you reshape the dough into small even rectangles. At this point the dough can be stored in the freezer for up to 1 month.

To bake, preheat the oven to 200ºC / 400ºF.

Evenly space the cookies on baking sheets lined with parchment paper 2.5 cm / 1 inch apart. Allow the dough to come to room temperature before baking.

Bake for 8—10 minutes.

These cookies keep well for 2—3 days stored in a sealed container.

BISCOTTI AL MAIS
CORNMEAL COOKIES

These cookies feature the taste of dry corn that is cultivated in Italy. We love Mulino della Langa Marino, a family run grainery in Piemonte, because their flour, farro and corn are exceptional and always freshly stone ground. We re-grind their delicious polenta di mais in our spice mill to make it finer for this recipe. We serve these simple cookies alongside baked or poached apples for dessert. They are also delicious with a glass of Barolo.

200 g / 1½ cup + 1 tsp finely ground cornmeal

200 g / 1⅓ cups + 2 tbsp all-purpose flour

8 g / 2 tsp baking powder

3 g / 1½ tsp ground cinnamon

1 g / ½ tsp ground cloves

Pinch of salt

150 g / ⅔ cup + 1 tsp butter

140 g / ⅔ cup + 1 tsp granulated sugar

2 large eggs, lightly beaten

13 g / 2 tbsp granulated sugar, for coating

Sift together the cornmeal, flour, baking powder, spices and salt in a medium-size mixing bowl.

Cream the butter, sugar and eggs at high speed. Reduce the speed to low, add the dry ingredients and mix until well combined. Cover the dough with plastic film and refrigerate for 30 minutes.

Lightly dust a work surface with flour and roll the dough out to an even 5 mm / ¼ inch thickness. Cut out preferred shapes with cookie cutters, re-roll the scraps and repeat. At this point the cookies can be layered between parchment paper, wrapped well in plastic film and stored in the freezer for up to 2 weeks. Allow the dough to come to room temperature before baking.

To bake, preheat the oven to 180°C / 350°F.

Coat 1 side of each cookie in the reserved granulated sugar. Transfer the cookies to cookie sheets lined with parchment paper, leaving 2.5 cm / 1 inch between each cookie.

Bake for 15 minutes, until the edges are golden.

These cookies keep for up to 1 week in a sealed container.

BISCOTTI INTEGRALI AL MIELE
WHOLE WHEAT HONEY COOKIES

YIELDS 36 COOKIES

This simple "milk" cookie is made with whole wheat flour and sweetened with honey. It is nutritious and meant to be eaten for breakfast dipped into a caffè latte.

90 g / ½ cup + 2 tbsp all-purpose flour

90 g / ½ cup + 2 tbsp whole wheat flour

2 g / ½ tsp baking powder

60 ml / 4 tbsp honey

90 ml / 6 tbsp olive oil

5 ml / 1 tsp vanilla extract

1 large egg

Granulated sugar, for coating

Preheat the oven to 180°C / 350°F.

Sift the flours and baking powder together in a small bowl. Combine the honey, olive oil, vanilla and egg in a medium-size bowl. Add the dry ingredients to the wet ingredients and stir until the dough is well combined.

Transfer the dough to a pastry bag with a 2.5-cm / ½-inch round tip. Pipe 2.5-cm / 2-inch strips onto cookie sheets lined with parchment paper, leaving 2.5 cm / 1 inch between each cookie. Sprinkle the cookies with granulated sugar.

Bake for 8 minutes.

These cookies store very well for up to 2 weeks in a sealed container.

TOZZETTI ALLE NOCCIOLE

HAZELNUT COOKIES

———

YIELDS 40 COOKIES

Tozzetti are traditional dry cookies that are found in every bakery in Rome. On their own they taste ordinary, but dipped into a sweet wine they make complete sense and are delicious. Pina Pasquantonio, AAR's sommelier, recommends Stillato di Principe Pallavicini.

105 g / 4 oz hazelnuts

470 g / 3¼ cups + 2 tbsp all-purpose flour

200 g / 1 cup sugar

9 g / 2¼ tsp baking powder

1 g / ¼ tsp salt

4 large eggs, lightly beaten

105 g / ½ cup unsalted butter

Preheat the oven to 150ºC / 300ºF.

Spread the hazelnuts evenly on a sheet pan and toast for 10 minutes, or until the skins begin to split. While the nuts are still warm, place them inside a clean tea towel. Gather the towel into a secure bundle and roll the nuts in a circular motion to loosen and remove some of the skins, and with them any extra bitterness. Lift the nuts out of the towel, leaving behind the skin, and transfer them to a cutting board. Coarsely chop the nuts by hand; the pieces should be large and irregular in size.

Reset the oven to 180ºC / 350ºF.

Combine the flour, sugar, baking powder and salt. Add the eggs and mix at low speed until incorporated. Then add the butter and continue to mix until all the ingredients are well combined.

Transfer the dough to a clean work surface and knead in the chopped hazelnuts by hand. Divide the dough into 5 equal pieces and form each portion into a log 3.5 cm / 1½ inches in diameter. Transfer the logs to a cookie sheet lined with parchment paper, leaving 5 cm /

2 inches between each one. Gently press each log to flatten slightly.

Bake the logs for 25 minutes, or until golden and slightly firm to the touch.

Once cool, transfer the cookie logs to a cutting board and cut them into approximately 2-cm / ¾-inch slices with a serrated knife. Lay cookies flat on cookie sheets lined with parchment paper and bake for 20 minutes, until golden brown.

These cookies will keep well in a sealed container for up to 6 weeks.

LINGUE DI GATTO
CAT'S TONGUE COOKIES

———

These delicate cookies pair well with panna cotta or can be sandwiched with chocolate ganache as part of a special mixed cookie plate.

60 g / 3 tbsp + 2 tsp butter

90 g / ⅓ cup + 2 tbsp granulated sugar

2 egg whites, lightly beaten

2.5 ml / ½ tsp vanilla extract

70 g / ½ cup all-purpose flour

1 g / ¼ tsp salt

Preheat the oven to 200ºC / 400ºF.

Cream the butter and sugar at high speed until light and fluffy. Add the egg whites and vanilla and mix at medium speed until well incorporated.

Sift the flour and salt and add them to the butter mixture. Continue to mix at low speed until well combined.

Transfer the batter into a medium pastry bag with a small round tip. Pipe the dough into 9-cm / 3-inch strips onto cookie sheets lined with parchment paper, leaving 2.5 cm / 1 inch between each cookie.

Bake for 8—10 minutes, until golden brown.

These cookies are best eaten freshly baked.

SAVOIARDI

LADYFINGERS

YIELDS 48 COOKIES

Chris Boswell, RSFP sous chef, loves tiramisu and is constantly trying to perfect his recipe. These cookies, a key component of tiramisu, were first prepared by Lisa Costa, RSFP intern '10. The recipe is inspired by Ada Boni's The Talisman Cookbook. *These ladyfingers are light and airy—ideal for tiramisu—for which they are quickly soaked in strong espresso, layered between sweetened mascarpone and topped with a dense layer of cocoa powder.*

6 egg yolks

5 ml / 1 tsp vanilla extract

145 g / 5¼ oz sugar

90 g / 2¼ oz flour

6 g / 1 tsp salt

6 egg whites

38 g / ¼ cup confectioners' sugar, for coating

25 g / 1½ tbsp granulated sugar

Pre-heat the oven to 190ºC / 375ºF.

Beat the egg yolks, vanilla and sugar together until pale and foamy. Combine the flour and salt and fold into the egg-sugar mixture until smooth. Beat the egg whites at medium speed until firm peaks form and gradually fold this into the egg yolk mixture.

Transfer the batter to a pastry bag and using a small round tip pipe about 7.5-cm / 3-inch-long ladyfingers onto cookie sheets lined with parchment paper, leaving 2.5 cm / 1 inch between each cookie.

Combine the confectioners' and granulated sugars and sift this mixture over the ladyfingers. Let them stand for 10 minutes. Sprinkle again with the sugar mixture. Let them stand for 5 minutes.

Bake for 10–12 minutes, until golden brown.

These cookies can be made up to 1 week in advance and stored in a sealed container in a cool dry place.

AMARETTI MELILLI
ALMOND MACAROONS FROM MELILLI

YIELDS 30 COOKIES

Mirella developed this recipe in the RSFP kitchen working with sous chef Chris Boswell. The goal was to achieve an ideal bittersweet balance. These amaretti are soft and chewy and made in the style of cookies from Mirella's hometown, Melilli, in Sicily.

280 g / 10 oz raw almonds

40 g / 1½ oz bitter almonds (see footnote)

200 g / 1 cup granulated sugar

Grated zest of 1 lemon

3 egg whites, lightly beaten

Preheat the oven to 200°C / 400°F.

Grind the almonds and sugar in a food processor until the texture is fine and sandy. Transfer the almond-sugar mixture to a medium-size mixing bowl. Mix in the lemon zest and egg whites.

Transfer the dough to a clean work surface. Lightly wet the tips of your fingers with water and shape the dough into 30 small balls (20 g / ¾ oz). Transfer the balls to cookie sheets lined with parchment paper, spacing them 2 cm / ¾ inch apart.

Leave the cookies out at room temperature for 1 hour to allow a crust to form before baking.

Bake for 10–15 minutes, until golden.

These cookies keep for up to 1 week in a sealed container.

* Bitter almonds are not available in the United States as they contain traces of cyanide and can be lethal if consumed in large quantities. Apricot or peach kernels of the same genus can be substituted for bitter almonds.

BISCOTTI LUCIA

LUCIA'S COOKIES

———

YIELDS 28 COOKIES

This recipe comes from Mirella's friend, Lucia Gulino of Siracusa, Sicily. There are many variations of Sicilian cookies using almonds, sugar, egg whites and lemon that can take fanciful forms. At the Academy, Mirella shapes these cookies into small balls and tops them with a blanched almond. They are simply superb.

250 g / 9 oz blanched almonds

200 g / 1 cup granulated sugar

2 g / 1 tsp ground cinnamon

1 g / ½ tsp grated lemon zest

1½ egg whites, lightly beaten

28 whole blanched almonds

Preheat the oven to 180ºC / 350ºF.

Pulse the almonds and sugar in a food processor until the almonds are chopped medium fine. Transfer the nut-sugar mixture to a medium-size mixing bowl. Add the cinnamon and lemon zest and mix well. Gently fold in the lightly beaten egg whites until well incorporated.

Roll the dough into 28 small balls (18 g / ¾ oz) and top each cookie with a blanched almond. Transfer the cookies to cookie sheets lined with parchment paper, spacing them 2 cm / ¾ inch apart.

Bake for 10 minutes. The cookies will be light in color and will form a nice crust as they cool.

These cookies will keep for up to 2 weeks in a sealed container.

BISCOTTI ALLE MANDORLE AMARE
BITTER ALMOND COOKIES

The almond trees growing near the Aurelian wall are the first fruit-bearing trees to bloom in the Bass Garden. Mirella learned to make a version of these cookies at Pasticceria Leonardi di Peruch in Siracusa, Sicily.

87 g / 3 oz raw blanched bitter almonds (see footnote)

500 g / 18 oz raw blanched almonds

225 g / 1 cup + 2 tbsp granulated sugar

5 ml / 1 tsp vanilla extract

40 ml / 2 tbsp + 2 tsp honey

Grated zest of 1 lemon

4 egg whites

250 g / 1⅔ cups confectioners' sugar, for coating

Preheat the oven to 180ºC / 350ºF.

In a food processor, finely grind the bitter and sweet almonds with 50 g / 2 tbsp of the sugar. The sugar provides grist for the almonds and prevents the nuts from becoming an oily paste.

Combine the almond-sugar mixture with the rest of the ingredients except for the confectioners' sugar in a medium-size mixing bowl. Mix with your hands until well combined. The dough should be soft and pliable and hold its shape.

Sprinkle the confectioners' sugar on a clean work surface. Pinch and roll the dough into 50 balls. Roll each ball in the confectioners' sugar and form into small sticks 7 cm / 2½ inches long and 1 cm / 1/3 inch in diameter. Gently form each stick into the shape of an N. Transfer the cookies to sheet pans lined with parchment paper, leaving 2 cm / ¾ inch between each cookie.

Bake for 10 minutes. Turn off the heat, open the door of the oven and leave the cookies for another 2 minutes to finish baking.

These cookies keep well in a sealed container for up to 2 weeks.

* Bitter almonds are not available in the United States as they contain traces of cyanide and can be lethal if consumed in large quantities. Apricot or peach kernels of the same genus can be substituted for bitter almonds.

DITA DI FATA
FAIRY FINGERS

———

YIELDS 36 COOKIES

Mirella brought us this recipe. Lightly flavored with orange flower water, they are pretty irresistible when dusted with confectioners' sugar.

80 g / ½ cup + 1 tbsp
all-purpose flour

60 g / ⅓ cup + 1 tbsp
confectioners' sugar

150 g / 5½ oz almonds,
finely ground

Pinch of salt

100 g / ⅓ cup + 2 tbsp butter

1 egg yolk

10 ml / 2 tsp orange flower water

50 g / ⅓ cup confectioners' sugar,
for coating

Combine the flour, confectioners' sugar, ground almonds and salt in a medium-size mixing bowl. Grate the chilled butter into the flour-nut mixture, using the large holes of a box grater. Rub the butter and flour nut mixture together with your fingers until it forms a crumbly consistency. Add the orange flour water and continue to gently work the dough until it comes together and forms a ball. Wrap the dough first in parchment paper, then plastic film and refrigerate for 30 minutes.

Preheat the oven to 180°C / 350°F.

Transfer the dough to a lightly floured work surface. Pinch off 10-g / ¼-oz pieces of dough and roll each ball between your hands to form 5-cm / 2-inch sticks.

Transfer the cookies to cookie sheets lined with parchment paper, spaced 2.5 cm / 1 inch apart.

Bake for 10–12 minutes until golden brown.

Once cool, generously dust with confectioners' sugar.

These cookies keep for 1 week in a sealed container.

PAIN D'AMANDE

ALMOND WAFER COOKIES

———

YIELS 90 COOKIES

Pain d'amande *are a signature cookie of the Chez Panisse pastry department and our version is now part of the RSFP repertoire. They are wonderfully crunchy and the perfect accompaniment to a bowl of buffalo milk gelato topped with sugared strawberries and a splash of prosecco.*

80 ml / 5 tbsp + 1 tsp water

110 g / ½ cup butter

2 g / 1 tsp ground cinnamon

300 g / 1½ cups Demerara sugar

140 g / 4½ oz slivered raw almonds

300 g / 2 cups + 2 tbsp all-purpose flour

Pinch of baking soda

Pinch of salt

Warm the water, butter and cinnamon in a 2-liter / 2-quart saucepan over low heat (do not allow it to boil). Once the butter has melted, remove from heat.

Once the liquid has cooled, transfer it to a large mixing bowl and gently stir in the sugar and nuts.

Sift the flour, baking soda and salt in a medium-size bowl. Gradually add the dry ingredients to the wet ingredients, mixing with a spatula until they are well combined and form a stiff dough. Shape the dough into two rectangular tiles 12 x 30 x 2 cm / 5 x 12 x ¾ inches. Wrap each tile first in parchment paper and then plastic film and refrigerate for 30 minutes. At this point, the dough can be stored in the freezer for up to 2 months.

To bake, preheat the oven to 160ºC / 325ºF.

Slice each tile into uniformly thin slices .5 cm x 2 inches. Evenly space the cookies on cookie sheets lined with parchment paper, leaving 4 cm / 2 inches between each cookie. Bake for 10–15 minutes or until they are a deep golden color. The cookies will crisp up as they cool.

Once baked, these cookies will keep in a sealed container for up to 1 week.

BISCOTTI ALLE NOCCIOLE
HAZELNUT BUTTER COOKIES

YIELDS 36 COOKIES

These rich and buttery cookies are made decadent with the addition of chopped hazelnuts. Hazelnuts are cultivated extensively in Lazio and have long been a staple in Roman desserts.

36 whole hazelnuts

225 g / 1⅔ cups all-purpose flour

1 g / ½ tsp ground cinnamon

Pinch of salt

225 g / 1 cup + 1 tbsp butter

140 g / ⅔ cup + 1 tsp granulated sugar

200 g / 7 oz hazelnuts

60 g / 3 tbsp granulated sugar, for coating

Preheat the oven to 150°C / 300°F.

Spread the hazelnuts evenly on a sheet pan and toast for 10 minutes, or until the skins begin to split. While the nuts are still warm, place them inside a clean tea towel. Gather the towel into a secure bundle and roll the nuts in a circular motion to loosen and remove some of the skins, and with them any extra bitterness. Lift the nuts out of the towel, leaving behind the skin, and transfer to a food processor. Pulse the toasted hazelnuts in the food processor until coarsely chopped.

Sift the flour, cinnamon and a pinch of salt in a medium-size mixing bowl.

Cream the butter and sugar until light and fluffy. Add the flour mixture and work the dough until it is even and smooth. Gently fold in the chopped hazelnuts without over-mixing the dough. Cover the dough in plastic film and refrigerate for 30 minutes.

Remove the dough from the refrigerator and form it into 36 small balls 16 g / ½ oz each. Transfer the cookies to cookie sheets lined with parchment paper, leaving 2.5 cm / ¾ inch between each cookie. Place 1 whole hazelnut in the center of each cookie and sprinkle them with the remaining 60 grams / 3 tbsp of granulated sugar.

Bake for 12 minutes, until golden brown.

These cookies are best eaten freshly baked.

BRUTTI MA BUONI

UGLY BUT GOOD COOKIES

————

YIELD 32-35 COOKIES

These cookies are inspired by Oretta Zanini de Vita's book The Food of Rome and Lazio, *which is an important reference book in the AAR kitchen. After the lunch rush and before the dinner menu meeting, the entire kitchen crew lines up at the Academy Bar for a coffee, a brief chat and a cookie.* Brutti ma buoni *is a sentimental favorite for many of the RSFP interns.*

500 g / 18 oz hazelnuts

2 egg whites

250 g / 1¼ cups granulated sugar

15 ml / 1 tbsp vanilla extract

10 g / 1 tbsp all-purpose flour

Grated zest of 1 lemon

Preheat the oven to 150°C / 300°F.

Spread the hazelnuts evenly on a sheet pan and toast for 10 minutes, or until the skins begin to split. While the nuts are still warm, place them inside a clean tea towel. Gather the towel into a secure bundle and roll the nuts in a circular motion to loosen and remove some of the skins, and with them any extra bitterness. Lift the nuts out of the towel, leaving behind the skins, and transfer them to a cutting board. Coarsely chop the nuts by hand; the pieces should be irregular in size.

Adjust the oven to 180°C / 350°F.

Beat the egg whites at high speed. When they begin to appear glossy and form soft peaks, add the sugar in a slow steady stream while continuing to mix at high speed. Add the vanilla extract once the sugar has been incorporated and the mixture forms stiff peaks.

Combine the nuts, flour and lemon zest in a medium-size bowl. Gently fold the egg whites into the nut mixture with a spatula. Use a teaspoon to drop mounds of the meringue-nut mixture onto cookie sheets lined with parchment paper, leaving 4 cm / 1½ inches between each cookie.

Bake for 10 minutes. After 10 minutes turn off the oven, open the door and leave the cookies there for 5 minutes. Remove the cookies from the oven; put them on a rack to continue cooling. Use a metal spatula to separate each cookie from the parchment.

These cookies keep well for 1 week in a sealed container stored in a cool dry place.

BISCOTTI CON NOCI E MARMELLATA

WALNUT JAM COOKIES

———

These delicate thumbprint jam cookies feature the RSFP jams made from plums, apricots and quinces that we harvest in the Bass Garden.

175 grams / 7 oz walnuts

110 grams / ½ cup butter

50 grams / ¼ cup granulated sugar

2.5 ml / ½ tsp vanilla extract

150 grams / 1 cup + 1 tbsp sifted all-purpose flour

125 grams / ½ cup thick jam

Preheat the oven to 150°C / 300°F.

Spread the walnuts evenly on a cookie sheet and toast for 10 minutes. While the nuts are still warm, transfer them to a clean tea towel. Gather the towel into a secure bundle and roll them in a circular motion to loosen and remove some of the skins. Transfer 75 g / 3¼ oz of the walnuts to a food processor, leaving behind the skins. Pulse the toasted nuts in the food processor with 1 tablespoon of sugar until they are evenly chopped. Finely chop the remaining nuts by hand and set them aside in a small bowl.

Cream the butter and until light and fluffy. Add the vanilla extract, sifted flour and the nut-sugar mixture and mix until well combined. Wrap the dough in plastic film and refrigerate for 1 hour.

Take the dough out of the refrigerator and roll into 40 balls 12 g / ½ oz each. Roll each ball in the reserved finely chopped walnuts. Use the tip of your finger to create a small depression in each cookie that later will be filled with jam.

To bake, reset or preheat the oven to 180°C / 350°F.

Place the cookies on cookie sheets lined with parchment paper, leaving 2.5 cm / 1 inch between each cookie. Bake for 10–12 minutes, until golden brown.

Once the cookies have cooled completely, fill each cookie with 7 ml / ½ teaspoon of thick jam.

These cookies are best eaten freshly baked.

PALLE DI NEVE
SNOWBALL COOKIES

YIELDS 80 COOKIES

These cookies melt in your mouth with most of the sweetness coming from the confectioners' sugar coating. When we were photographing the cover of this book it began to snow, the first large snowfall in Rome in twenty-five years. From high up on the Gianicolo looking out over Rome, the snow-capped domes looked remarkably like the delicate white cookies before us, more commonly known as Russian teacakes.

140 g / 5 oz hazelnuts

300 g / 2 cups + 2 tbsp all-purpose flour

230 g / 1 cup + 1 tbsp butter

85 g / ¼ cup + 3 tbsp granulated sugar

5 ml / 1 tsp vanilla extract

5 ml / 1 tsp water

325 g / 2 cups + 3 tbsp confectioners' sugar, for coating

Preheat the oven to 150°C / 300°F.

Spread the hazelnuts evenly on a sheet pan and toast for 10 minutes, or until the skins begin to split. While the nuts are still warm, place them inside a clean tea towel. Gather the towel into a secure bundle and roll the nuts in a circular motion to loosen and remove some of the skins, and with them any extra bitterness. Lift the nuts out of the towel, leaving behind the skin, and transfer to a food processor. Pulse the toasted hazelnuts in the food processor with 2 tablespoons of the flour until they create an even, sandy texture.

Cream the butter and sugar until light and fluffy. Add the vanilla extract and water and mix until well incorporated. Add the ground hazelnut mixture and remaining flour and continue to mix on low speed until the dough forms a ball. Wrap the dough in plastic film and refrigerate for at least 30 minutes.

Remove the dough from the refrigerator and form into 80 balls 9 g / ⅓ oz each. At this point, the balls of unbaked cookie dough can be stored in a sealed container and kept frozen for up to 1 month.

To bake, reset or preheat the oven to 180°C / 350°F.

Place the balls on cookie sheets lined with parchment paper, leaving 3.5 cm / 1½ inches between each cookie. Allow the dough to come to room temperature before baking. Bake for 10–12 minutes.

Once the cookies have entirely cooled, roll them in confectioners' sugar one or two times until they are completely covered and look like little snowballs.

These cookies are best eaten freshly baked.

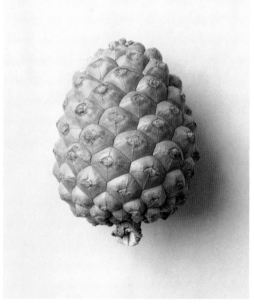

PINOLATE
PINE NUT COOKIES

YIELDS 20 COOKIES

Many of the ancient roads leading into Rome are lined with towering umbrella pines. In the late fall grandparents and grandchildren forage in the Villa Doria Pamphili for pine cones and patiently harvest the pignoli *nuts.* Pinolatti *are biscottini piccolini, small delicate cookies, and have pine nuts inside and out.*

200 g / 7 oz pine nuts	Preheat the oven to 150°C / 300°F.
85 g / 3 oz blanched almonds	Spread the pine nuts evenly on a cookie sheet and toast for approximately 10 minutes or until lightly golden. Let cool before using. Pulse the almonds with the granulated sugar and 50 g / ⅓ cup of the total pine nuts in a food processor to create a fine sandy texture. Transfer the nut and sugar mixture to a medium-size mixing bowl. Add the lemon zest, vanilla and egg white and mix well. Cover the dough with plastic film and refrigerate for 30 minutes.
85 g / ¼ cup + 3 tbsp granulated sugar	
2 g / ½ tsp grated lemon zest	
2 ml / ¼ tsp vanilla extract	
1 egg white, lightly beaten	

Form the dough into cherry-size balls (10 g / ⅓ oz) and roll each ball in the remainder of the toasted pine nuts, pressing them gently into the dough.

To bake, adjust or preheat the oven to 160°C / 325°F.

Evenly space the cookies on cookie sheets lined with parchment paper, leaving 2 cm / 1½ inches between each cookie. Bake for 9–10 minutes, until golden brown.

These cookies are best eaten freshly baked, but will keep for up to 1 week in a sealed container.

BISCOTTI AL PISTACCHIO

PISTACHIO COOKIES

YIELDS 45-50 COOKIES

This is one of Mirella's best Sicilian cookie recipes. Ruth Reichl, the former editor of Gourmet, tweeted about them after tasting one on her visit to the AAR in the summer of 2009. Tender and delicious, these sugar-coated pistachio cookies are brilliantly green inside.

500 g / 4⅓ cups raw pistachios

200 g / 1 cup granulated sugar

25 g / 1 tbsp honey

5 ml / 1 tsp vanilla extract

Grated zest of half a lemon (approximately 20 ml / 1½ tbsp)

3½ oz egg whites

150 g / 1 cup confectioners' sugar

50 (2 oz) whole raw pistachios for garnishing

Preheat the oven to 180°C / 350°F.

Pulse the pistachios in a food processor with half of the measured granulated sugar (100 g / ½ cup) until the nuts are finely chopped.

Combine the ground pistachio-sugar mixture with the honey, vanilla and lemon zest in a large mixing bowl. Slowly add the egg whites, mixing until the dough is well combined and soft. At this point, add the additional 100 g / ½ cup of granulated sugar and mix gently. The dough will be soft but not sticky.

Form the dough into small balls (16 g / ½ oz) and roll them in the confectioners' sugar to coat well. Transfer the balls to cookie sheets lined with parchment paper, leaving 3 cm / 1¼ inches between each cookie. Gently press a pistachio into the center of each cookie.

Bake for 15—18 minutes, until the edges of each cookie are golden.

These cookies can be stored in a sealed container for up to 2 weeks.

AMARETTI CON PISTACCHI E ARANCIA
MACAROONS WITH PISTACHIOS AND ORANGE

YIELDS 25-30 COOKIES

Amaretti are classic Italian cookies traditionally made with bitter almonds and lemon zest. We discovered this interesting variation, which uses pistachios and bitter orange zest.

50 g / ⅓ cup + 1 tsp
all-purpose flour

Pinch of salt

100 g / 3½ oz raw pistachios

100 g / ½ cup + 25 g / 2 tbsp
granulated sugar

Grated zest of 1 Seville orange

3 egg whites

25 g / 1 oz confectioners' sugar,
for coating

25 g / 1 oz pistachios,
finely chopped, for coating

Preheat the oven to 180°C / 350°F.

Sift the flour and salt in a medium-size mixing bowl.

Grind the pistachios, 100 g / ½ cup sugar and orange zest in the bowl of a food processor until the mixture is fine and sandy. Add this nut-sugar mix to the flour and mix well.

Beat the egg whites at medium speed. When the egg whites form soft peaks, increase the speed and slowly pour in the remaining 25 g / 2 tbsp granulated sugar. Continue to mix until the peaks are shiny and firm. Gently fold in the flour-pistachio mixture to incorporate.

Use a teaspoon to drop small mounds of batter onto cookie sheets lined with parchment paper, evenly spacing the cookies 4 cm / 1½ inches apart. Sprinkle the remaining 20 grams of finely chopped pistachios over the tops of the cookies.

Bake for 10–12 minutes, or until the cookies are golden brown and firm to the touch.

Once they are completely cool, carefully remove them from the parchment paper with a metal spatula and dust with confectioners' sugar.

These cookies will keep for 2–3 days in a sealed container.

FAVE DOLCI
FAVA BEAN COOKIES

———

YIELDS 70 BEAN-SIZE COOKIES

These little cookies are the size, shape and color of spring fava beans. We first served them on a candy plate for the annual spring Cortile Dinner that celebrates the Rome Prize Winners becoming Fellows of the American Academy in Rome. The original recipe came from Oretta Zanini de Vita's book The Food of Rome *and* Lazio *and uses ground almonds in place of pistachios. We use a combination of both, which is what makes these cookies resemble dried fava beans.*

100 g / 3½ oz raw pistachios

100 g / ½ cup granulated sugar

100 g / ⅔ cup + 1 tbsp all-purpose flour

30 g / 2 tbsp + 1 tsp butter

Grated zest of 1 lemon

1 large egg

Finely grind the nuts and sugar in the bowl of a food processor until they are the texture of fine sand. Combine the flour, butter, egg, lemon zest and nut-sugar mixture until the dough begins to form a ball. Wrap the dough in plastic film and transfer to the refrigerator for 30 minutes.

Preheat the oven to 160ºC / 325ºF.

Roll the dough into 70 small balls (5 g / ⅙ oz), then gently press the side of each cookie with the tip of your finger so they resemble little fava beans.

Transfer the cookies to cookie sheets lined with parchment paper spacing them 2 cm / ¾ inch apart. Bake for 10 minutes, then turn off the oven, open the door and allow the cookies to remain in the oven for another 2 minutes.

These cookies keep well for 2−3 days in a tightly covered container.

BISCOTTI CREMA D'ARACHIDI

PEANUT BUTTER COOKIES

YIELDS 45 COOKIES

We have found that most Italians loathe crema d'arachidi, but the RSFP keeps it in stock for our American Fellows. Norm Roberson, who was the AAR gatekeeper for twenty-one years, asked us to make peanut butter cookies, his childhood favorite.

110 g / ½ cup butter

375 g / 1½ cups chunky peanut butter

150 g / ¾ cup granulated sugar

120 g / ¾ cup brown sugar

1 large egg + 1 yolk

265 g / 1¾ cups + 2 tbsp all-purpose flour

15 g / 1 tbsp baking powder

Pinch of salt

Cream the butter, peanut butter, granulated sugar and brown sugar together at medium speed for 4 minutes. Add the egg and yolk and continue to mix until well incorporated.

Sift the flour, baking powder and salt in a bowl. Gradually add the dry ingredients to the wet mixture on low speed until a dough forms. Cover the dough with plastic film and refrigerate for 30 minutes.

Remove the dough from the refrigerator and divide it in three. Roll each portion into logs 4 cm / 1½ inches in diameter. Wrap the logs first in parchment paper, then plastic film and place in the freezer for at least 2 hours or up to 1 month.

To bake, preheat the oven to 160°C / 325°F.

Slice each log into thin slices approximately .5 cm / ¼ inch thick. Evenly space the cookies on cookie sheets lined with parchment paper, leaving 3 cm / 1½ inches between each cookie. Allow the dough to come to room temperature before baking. Bake for 8–10 minutes. The cookies will be soft when they come out of the oven and will firm up as they cool.

These cookies are best eaten freshly baked.

BISCOTTI DI MIELE

HONEY COOKIES

———

YIELDS 60 COOKIES

The Academy has wonderful organic raw milk delivered twice a week. Our dairy farmer also cultivates bees and we buy his wildflower honey. Biscotti di miele stands out in our repertoire because it is neither American nor Italian; its origin is Swiss. This is a very crunchy cookie that is meant to be dunked in a cup of milky bergamot tea, which enhances the natural floral flavor of the honey.

400 g / 1 cup + 2 tbsp honey

255 g / 1¼ cups + 1 tsp granulated sugar

12 g / 2 tsp baking soda

30 ml / 2 tbsp grappa

120 g / ⅔ cup candied orange peel, finely chopped

130 g / 4½ oz raw almonds, finely chopped

5 g / ½ tsp ground cinnamon

5 g / ½ tsp ground cloves

Pinch freshly grated nutmeg

536 g / 3¾ cups + 1 tbsp all-purpose flour

1 cup confectioners' sugar for icing

Heat the honey and sugar in a heavy-bottomed 2-liter / 2-quart pot over low heat and cook, stirring frequently, until the sugar dissolves. Set aside to cool.

Mix the baking soda and grappa at low speed until the baking soda is dissolved, then add the cooled honey. Add the candied orange peel, chopped almonds, cinnamon, cloves and nutmeg and continue to mix. Gradually add the flour until the mixture forms a firm ball. You may need to transfer the dough to a clean work surface to knead in the last cup of flour by hand. Cover the dough with plastic film and set aside in a cool place overnight (do not refrigerate).

To bake, preheat the oven to 180°C / 350°F.

Transfer the dough to a lightly floured work surface and divide it in two. Roll out each portion to an even .66-cm / ¼-inch thickness. Cut out your preferred shapes with cookie cutters, re-roll the scraps and repeat. With a sharp knife, deeply score each cookie to create the pattern of your choice. This will prevent the cookies from rising unevenly.

Transfer the cut-out cookies to cookie sheets lined with parchment paper and bake for 12–15 minutes, until lightly browned.

Mix together confectioners' sugar and 45 ml / 3 tablespoons of water in a bowl until smooth. While the cookies are still warm, brush a thin layer of the frosting on to each one. Set aside to cool completely.

These cookies will keep well in a sealed container for up to 3 months.

BISCOTTI DI MIELE E CARDAMOMO

HONEY AND CARDAMOM COOKIES

———

YIELDS 35 COOKIES

On Saturdays we often cook a lunch menu that is inspired by a craving for something other than Italian food. Most often it is Turkish, Lebanese or Israeli, as our pantry ingredients easily lend themselves to eastern Mediterranean cooking. If time allows, we also make a special dessert. These delicate cookies are lightly scented with honey, rosewater and cardamom and delicious with yogurt and pistachios.

350 g / 2½ cups all-purpose flour

Sift together the flour, baking soda, cardamom and salt in a medium-size mixing bowl.

3 g / ½ tsp baking soda

6 g / 2 tsp ground cardamom

Mix together the rose water, honey and milk in a small bowl.

Pinch of salt

2.5 ml / ½ tsp rose water

60 ml / 4 tbsp honey

2 tbsp milk

Cream the butter and sugar, then add the egg and mix until smooth and fluffy. Add the dry ingredients to the butter mixture, then add the liquid ingredients and mix until combined. Wrap the dough in plastic film and refrigerate for 30 minutes.

60 g / ¼ cup + 1 tsp butter

80 g / ⅓ cup + 1 tbsp granulated sugar

1 large egg

Remove the dough from the refrigerator and divide in two. On a lightly floured surface form each portion into logs 4 cm / 1½ inches in diameter. Wrap the logs first in parchment paper, then in plastic film and freeze for at least 1 hour or up to 2 weeks.

40 g / 4 tbsp confectioners' sugar for dusting

To bake, preheat the oven to 180°C / 350°F.

Slice the logs into 5-mm / ¼-inch-thick slices. Evenly space the cookies on cookie sheets lined with parchment paper, leaving 2 cm / ¾ inch between each cookie. Allow the dough to come to room temperature before baking.

Bake for 10–12 minutes, until the cookies are golden around the edges. While the cookies are still warm, generously dust them with sifted confectioners' sugar.

These cookies keep well in a sealed container for up to 1 week.

BISCOTTI ANZAC
ANZAC COOKIES

———

The recipe for these crunchy Australian cookies comes from Kat Grandage, whose husband, James Stone, was the chef for the Australian ambassador to Italy. James and Kat volunteered to help launch the RSFP in the earliest days. ANZAC is an acronym for Australia and N2 Army Corps who served together in Turkey in World War II.

140 g / 1 cup all-purpose flour

200 g / 1 cup granulated sugar

90 g / 1 cup unsweetened coconut

110 g / 1 cup + 3 tbsp rolled oats

Pinch of salt

120 g / ½ cup + 1 tbsp butter, melted

15 ml / 1 tbsp honey

60 ml / 4 tbsp boiling water

4 g / 1 tsp baking soda

Preheat oven to 160ºC / 325ºF.

Mix together the flour, sugar, coconut, oats and salt in a medium-size mixing bowl. Combine the melted butter, honey and boiling water in a separate bowl, then add the baking soda. Quickly add the wet ingredients to the dry ingredients and mix well.

Divide the dough in two and shape each portion into logs 3 cm / 1¼ inches in diameter. Slice each log into 1-cm / ½-inch slices. Evenly space the cookies on cookie sheets lined with parchment paper, leaving 2.5 cm / 1 inch between each cookie.

Bake for 12 minutes.

These cookies keep well for up to 1 month in a sealed container.

BACI DI COCCO
COCONUT MACAROONS

———

YIELDS 30-35 COOKIES

The original recipe for these coconut macaroons comes from David Lebovitz's excellent cookbook, Room for Dessert. *They are a perfect macaroon "kiss" and always sell out at the Academy Bar. They are joyfully delicious when baked a couple of minutes less, topped with a blanched almond and dipped in melted chocolate.*

4 egg whites

285 g / 1⅓ cups + 5 tsp granulated sugar

15 ml / 1 tablespoon honey

5 ml / 1 tsp vanilla extract

3 g / ½ tsp salt

225 g / 2½ cups unsweetened grated coconut

40 g / ¼ cup + 2 tsp all-purpose flour

Gently warm the egg whites, sugar, honey, vanilla and salt over low heat in a 3-liter / 3-quart saucepan. Once the sugar begins to melt and the mixture is warm to the touch, add the coconut and flour. Stir the mixture continuously with a wooden spoon for another 3–4 minutes until the mixture begins to brown and stick to the pan and appears dry.

Remove the macaroon mix from the heat and transfer to a shallow pan to cool completely. Once cool, cover the pan with plastic film and refrigerate for 30 minutes.

Remove the dough from the refrigerator and roll it into balls (22 g / 1 oz). At this point the cookies can be frozen for up to 1 month. To do this, first freeze the rolled balls on a cookie sheet lined with parchment paper. Once they have hardened, transfer them to a sealed container and store in the freezer until ready to use.

To bake, preheat the oven to 180ºC / 350ºF.

Evenly space the macaroons on cookie sheets lined with parchment paper, leaving 2.5 cm /

1 inch between each cookie. Allow the dough to come to room temperature before baking. Bake for 15–20 minutes, until golden brown.

These cookies can be stored in a sealed container for 2–3 days.

BISCOTTI AL LIMONE E PISTACCHIO

LEMON PISTACHIO SANDWICH COOKIES

———

YIELDS 30-35 COOKIES

We serve these cookies for special occasions such as the annual Fellows Tea hosted by the Academy's Director. In this recipe we showcase Pistacchi di Bronte *and* Limoni di Sorrento, *two exceptional southern Italian ingredients.*

100 g / 8 tbsp butter

125 g / ⅔ cup granulated sugar

1 large egg

Grated zest of 1 lemon

2 tbsp lemon juice

200 g / 1⅓ cups + 2 tbsp all-purpose flour

Pinch of salt

90 g / 3¾ oz raw pistachios, finely chopped

Lemon Icing:
150 g / 1 cup confectioners' sugar, sifted

37 ml / 2½ tbsp lemon juice

30 g / 1 oz raw pistachios, finely chopped, for coating

Beat the butter and sugar until light and fluffy. Add the egg, lemon zest and lemon juice and mix until well incorporated.

Combine the flour, salt and pistachios in a medium-size mixing bowl. Add the dry mixture to the butter-egg mixture and stir until well combined. Wrap the dough in plastic film and store in refrigerator for 30 minutes.

To bake, preheat the oven to 160ºC / 325ºF.

Lightly dust a work surface with flour and roll out the dough to an even 5-mm / ¼-inch thickness. Return the dough to the refrigerator for 10 minutes. With a cookie cutter of your choice cut out desired shapes, re-roll the scraps and repeat. Transfer cookies to cookie sheets lined with parchment paper leaving 2.5 cm / 1 inch between each cookie.

Bake for 12–15 minutes, until the edges of each cookie are golden brown.

To make the icing, combine the confectioners' sugar and lemon juice until smooth.

When the cookies are cool, create sandwiches by spreading a half-teaspoon of icing between two cookies. Spread thin layer icing on the top of each sandwich and sprinkle with finely chopped pistachios.

These cookies are best eaten freshly baked.

BISCOTTI LINZER

LINZER COOKIES

———

YIELDS 24 COOKIES

Toward the end of their stay at the Academy, RSFP interns have the opportunity to write and prepare a seasonal menu. The AAR community looks forward to these dinners to honor the hard work and commitment each stagista brings to the program. Peter Beck interned with the RSFP in 2008 while taking a gap year before college and made these delicious Linzer cookies for his dessert.

170 g / ¾ cups + 2 tsp butter

100 g / ½ cup granulated sugar

2½ ml / ½ tsp vanilla extract

260 g / 1¾ cups + 2 tbsp all-purpose flour, sifted

Pinch of salt

Confectioners' sugar for dusting

65 g / ¼ cup thick jam for filling

Cream the butter and sugar at high speed until light and fluffy, then add the vanilla. Combine flour and salt in a small bowl and add to the butter mixture; mix on medium speed until well combined. Wrap the dough in plastic film and refrigerate for at least 30 minutes.

Lightly dust your work surface with flour and roll the dough out to an even (5 mm / ¼ inch) thickness. Cut the dough into desired shapes with cookie cutters. Cut equal numbers of each shape so that you have pairs to make sandwiches. Cut 2.5-cm / 1-inch circles out of half the cookies for the jam filling to show through. Re-roll the scraps to cut more shapes.

Transfer cookies to cookie sheets lined with parchment paper, leaving 1.5 cm / ½ inch between each cookie. At this point cookies can be stored in the freezer, well wrapped, for up to 2 weeks.

To bake preheat the oven to 180ºC / 350ºF.

Allow the dough to come to room temperature before baking. Bake for 10—12 minutes, until the edges of each cookie are golden.

When the cookies are entirely cool, create sandwiches by spreading a half-teaspoon of jam on the bottom cookies. Dust the top cookies (those with the holes) with confectioners' sugar and place on top.

These cookies are best eaten freshly baked.

BISCOTTI DI ZUCCHERO

SUGAR COOKIES

YIELDS 35-40 COOKIES

In the fall of 2009 the RSFP welcomed visiting cook Camilla Houstoun from Darina Allen's Ballymaloe cookery school in County Cork, Ireland. On Halloween she organized a cookie decorating party for the Academy children. The maintenance crew cleverly crafted bat- and ghost-shaped cookie cutters out of tin cans. We have since used this simple 1-2-3 cookie recipe for many other occasions.

100 g / 1 cup all-purpose flour, sifted

200 g / ¾ cups + 3 tbsp salted butter (add a pinch of salt if using unsalted butter)

300 g / 1½ cups granulated sugar

Grate the chilled butter into the sifted flour using the large holes of a box grater. Rub the butter and flour together with your fingers until they form a sandy consistency. Add the sugar and combine with your hands until the dough forms a ball. If the dough is dry, knead it for a couple of minutes until it is pliable. Wrap the dough first in parchment paper, then plastic film and refrigerate for 30 minutes.

To bake, preheat the oven to 180°C / 350°F.

Lightly dust your work surface with flour and roll out the dough to an even 1 cm / ½ inch thickness. Cut out your preferred shapes with cookie cutters, re-roll the scraps and repeat.

Transfer the cookies to cookie sheets lined with parchment paper, leaving 2.5 cm / 1 inch between each. Bake for 7—10 minutes or until golden.

When the cookies have cooled, decorate with frosting. Or if you prefer, you can sprinkle the cookies with granulated sugar before baking.

These cookies keep well for 2—3 days in a sealed container.

BISCOTTI ALLA NOCE MOSCATA

NUTMEG COOKIES

These cookies are rich and buttery and highlight freshly grated nutmeg. They are perfect cookies for the afternoon tea. Mirella likes using a cookie press for speed and efficiency, but one can easily roll the dough into little balls and shape them into flowers.

300 g / 2 cups plus 2 tbsp all-purpose flour

1.5 g / 1½ tsp freshly grated nutmeg

Pinch of salt

250 g / 1 cup + 3 tbsp butter

60 g / 4 tbsp Robiola or cream cheese

1 egg yolk

150 g / ¾ cup granulated sugar

Freshly grated nutmeg for the tops of the cookies

Preheat the oven to 180°C / 350°F.

Sift the flour, nutmeg, and salt in a medium-size mixing bowl. Cream the butter, cheese, egg yolk and sugar. Add in the dry ingredients to the butter mixture and continue mixing until the ingredients are well incorporated.

Put the dough into the cookie press and extrude the cookies, using the disk shape of your choice, onto cookie sheets lined with parchment paper, leaving 2.5 cm / 1 inch between each cookie.

Bake for 12–15 minutes, until golden. Remove the cookies from the oven and grate fresh nutmeg over the cookies while they are still warm.

These cookies will keep in a sealed container for up to 2 days.

BISCOTTI AI DATTERI E NOCI
DATE AND WALNUT COOKIES

———

YIELDS 36 COOKIES

Giovanni Bernabei of San Giovanni Incarico, our favorite farmer, brings us 50-kilo bags of walnuts in their shells throughout the winter months. On rainy afternoons we entice the Fellows with hot chocolate and in return they shell the nuts. The RSFP mission is to nourish and support work and conviviality and this collaboration does just that.

100 g / ¾ cup all-purpose flour	Preheat the oven to 180°C / 350°F.
45 g / ⅓ cup farro flour	Sift the flours, cinnamon and salt in a medium-size mixing bowl.
1 g / ½ tsp ground cinnamon	
3 g / ½ tsp salt	Cream the butter and sugar until light and fluffy. Scrape down the sides of the bowl, add the egg and continue to mix until the egg is just incorporated. Add the dry ingredients and then gently mix in the dates and walnuts until evenly distributed.
60 g / ⅓ cup butter	
100 g / ½ cup granulated sugar	
1 large egg	
125 g / ⅔ cup dates, finely chopped	Use a tablespoon to drop mounds of dough approximately 16 g / ½ oz each onto cookie sheets lined with parchment paper, leaving 2.5 cm / 1 inch between each cookie. Place 1 walnut half in the center of each cookie.
75 g / ⅔ cup walnuts, coarsely chopped and lightly toasted	
36 walnut halves	Bake for 12–15 minutes, until golden brown. While the cookies are still warm, sift a generous amount of confectioners' sugar on top.
38 g / ¼ cup confectioners' sugar, for coating	
	These cookies will keep for 2–3 days in a sealed container.

BISCOTTI AI FICHI
FIG COOKIES

―――――

YIELDS 56 COOKIES

Fig cookies are a favorite of the Italian and American staff and this recipe was quickly adopted into our repertoire. The figs in the Bass Garden ripen in August when the Academy is closed and many Romans escape to the seaside. The AAR staff that work through the intense August heat are rewarded with the best figs of the season. Come September, there are a few figs left behind, which the new crop of Fellows are thrilled to discover and enjoy.

Fig filling:
400 g / 2 cups dried figs, roughly chopped

80 g / ⅓ cup + 1 tbsp granulated sugar

Grated zest of 2 oranges

1.25 ml / ¼ tsp vanilla extract

Cookie dough:
350 g / 2½ cups all-purpose flour

2 g / ½ tsp baking powder

1 g / ¼ tsp ground cinnamon

3 g / ½ tsp salt

90 g / 7 tbsp butter

130 g / ⅔ cup brown sugar

2.5 ml / ½ tsp vanilla extract

2 large eggs

To make the filling, combine the figs, sugar and orange zest in a 1-liter / 1-quart saucepan. Cover the figs with cold water and simmer for 30 minutes. Remove the mixture from the heat and when it has cooled, add the vanilla extract.

Sift the flour, baking powder, cinnamon and salt in a small bowl.

Cream the butter and sugar at high speed until light and fluffy. Add the vanilla extract and eggs, then reduce the speed and gently stir in the flour mixture until well combined. Wrap the dough in plastic film and refrigerate for 30 minutes.

Preheat oven to 160°C / 325°F.

Remove the dough from the refrigerator and divide it in two. On a lightly floured work surface, roll the dough into 30-cm / 12-inches x 8-cm / 3¼-inch rectangles. Trim the edges with a knife to ensure accurate measurements.

Divide the fig filling in half and spread it evenly down the middle of each rectangle. Fold over the sides of the rectangles to seal the logs. Turn the logs over so the seal is on the bottom. The logs should now measure 30 cm / 12 inches x 4 cm / 1¾ inches. Transfer the logs to cookie sheets lined with parchment paper.

Bake for 10−12 minutes, until lightly brown and firm to the touch.

Once cool, slice each rectangle into 3-cm / 1¼-inch pieces. These cookies will soften and keep for up to 3 days in a sealed container.

BISCOTTI DI FIOCCHI D'AVENA

OATMEAL RAISIN COOKIES

———

YIELDS 36 COOKIES

These oatmeal raisin cookies are favorites with everyone at the Academy. We often pack them in picnics that Fellows take to their studios when working intently on a project or on visits to archaeological sites.

100 g / 2/3 cup raisins

110 g / ½ cup butter

125 g / ½ cup + 2 tbsp granulated sugar

1 large egg + 1 yolk

15 ml / 1 tbsp mild honey

7.5 ml / ½ tbsp pure dark molasses

75 g / ¾ cup rolled oats

140 g / 1 cup all-purpose flour

1.5 g / ¼ tsp baking soda

1 g / ¼ tsp ground nutmeg

1 g / ½ tsp ground cinnamon

1 g / ¼ tsp salt

Soak the raisins in enough water to cover for 15 minutes. Drain and reserve.

Cream the butter and sugar at high speed until light and fluffy. Gradually add the whole egg and yolk to the butter mixture and mix well. Reduce the speed and add the honey, molasses, oats and raisins.

Sift together the flour, baking soda, nutmeg, cinnamon and salt in a medium-size mixing bowl. Add the dry ingredients to the wet mixture, continuing to mix on low speed until the dough comes together. Cover with plastic film and refrigerate for 30 minutes.

Remove the dough from the refrigerator and divide it in two. Roll each portion into logs 4 cm / 1½ inches in diameter. Wrap the logs first in parchment paper, then in plastic film and freeze for at least 2 hours or up to 1 month.

To bake, preheat the oven to 180°C / 350°F.

Slice the logs into .5-cm / ½-inch-thick slices. Evenly space the cookies on cookie sheets lined with parchment paper, leaving 3 cm / 1½ inches between each cookie. Allow the dough to come to room temperature before baking. Bake for 10–12 minutes, or until the edges of each cookie are golden.

These cookies are crisp and chewy when freshly baked but will soften when stored in a sealed container for up to 3 days.

BISCOTTI DI ZENZERO

GINGER COOKIES

———

We make these cookies for the annual Christmas play that the Fellows put on for children at the Academy. After the play ends and the presents have been passed out, the celebration begins. The community gathers around a large spread of holiday treats and each child finds a cookie with their name written in frosting. Sometimes the long Italian names require two cookies.

125 g / ½ cup + 1½ tbsp butter

90 g / ½ cup + 1 tbsp light brown sugar

.75 ml / 3 tbsp dark molasses

1 egg

310 g / 2¼ cups all-purpose flour

6 g / 1 tsp baking soda

3 g / ½ tsp salt

2 g / 1 tsp allspice

6 g / 1 tbsp ground ginger

2 g / 1 tsp ground cinnamon

Cream the butter and sugar until light and fluffy. Add the molasses and egg and mix well. In a medium-size mixing bowl, sift together the flour, baking soda, salt and spices. Add the dry ingredients to the butter mixture and continue mixing until well combined. Wrap the dough in plastic film and refrigerate for 30 minutes.

Lightly dust your work surface with flour and roll out the dough to an even (2 cm / ¼ inch) thickness. Cut out your preferred shapes with cookie cutters, re-roll the scraps and repeat. Transfer the cookies to cookie sheets lined with parchment paper, leaving 2.5 cm / 1 inch between each cookie. At this point the cookies can be wrapped well, layered between parchment paper and frozen for up to 2 weeks. Allow the dough to come to room temperature before baking.

To bake, preheat the oven to 180°C / 350°F.

Bake for 10—12 minutes.

These cookies keep well for up to 1 week in a sealed container.

BISCOTTI DI MARY PAT

MARY PAT'S GINGER MOLASSES COOKIES

———

YIELDS 35-40 COOKIES

Mary Pat Walsh proudly holds the title of the Rome Sustainable Food Project's first intern. She brought this delicious chewy cookie recipe to Rome and it has been an Academy favorite from the beginning.

150 g / 5½ oz butter

200 g / 1 cup granulated sugar

115 g / ⅓ cup dark molasses

1 large egg

395 g / 2¾ cups + 1 tbsp all-purpose flour

2 g / ½ tsp salt

12 g / 2 tsp baking soda

6 g / 1 tbsp ground ginger

2 g / ¾ tsp ground cloves

2 g / 1½ tsp ground cinnamon

100 g / ½ cup granulated sugar, for coating

Cream the butter and sugar at high speed until light and fluffy. Scrape down the sides of the bowl with a spatula and adjust the mixer to low speed. Add the molasses in a slow steady stream, then the egg. Continue to mix until well combined.

Sift the flour, salt, baking soda and spices in a medium-size bowl. Add the dry ingredients all at once to the wet mixture. Continue to mix on low speed until all the ingredients are well incorporated. Wrap the dough in plastic film and refrigerate for at least 30 minutes.

Remove the dough from the refrigerator and gently roll into 10-g / ¼-oz balls. At this point the balls of dough can be stored in the freezer for up to 2 months.

To bake, preheat the oven to 180°C / 350°F.

Coat each ball in the reserved sugar. Place on cookie sheets lined with parchment paper, leaving 3 cm / 1¼ inches between each. Allow the dough to come to room temperature before baking.

Bake for 10–12 minutes, until golden brown.

These cookies are best eaten freshly baked.

SNICKERDOODLES
SNICKERDOODLES

——————

YIELDS 80 SMALL COOKIES

Snickerdoodles are an old-fashioned American-style cookie. Soft and chewy with thin cinnamon-sugar crusts, they are a sentimental favorite with a glass of cold milk.

350 g / 1¾ cups granulated sugar

340 g / 1½ cups + 4 tsp unsalted butter

Vanilla extract

4 g / 2 tsp ground cinnamon

2 large eggs

400 g / 2¾ cups + 2 tbsp all-purpose flour

7 g / 2 tsp cream of tartar

6 g / 1 tsp baking soda

3 g / ¾ tsp salt

6 g / 3 tsp ground cinnamon, for coating

50 g / ¼ cup granulated sugar, for coating

Cream the sugar and butter together at high speed until light and fluffy. Add the vanilla and cinnamon and mix for 1 more minute. Add the eggs, 1 at a time, and mix until well incorporated.

Sift together the flour, cream of tartar, baking soda and salt in a medium-size mixing bowl. Add the dry ingredients to the butter mixture and mix on low speed until combined. Wrap the dough in plastic film and refrigerate for at least 30 minutes.

Remove the dough from the refrigerator and form into 80 balls (10 g / ⅓ oz). At this point, the balls of unbaked cookie dough can be stored in a sealed container and kept frozen for up to 1 month.

To bake, preheat oven to 190ºC / 375ºF.

Combine the remaining sugar and cinnamon in a small bowl. Roll each ball in the cinnamon-sugar mixture to coat and place them on cookie sheets lined with parchment paper, leaving 5 cm / 2 inches between each cookie.

Allow dough to come to room temperature before baking. Bake for 10–12 minutes, until golden.

BISCOTTI DI SIENA SPEZIATE
SIENA SPICE COOKIES

YIELDS APPROXIMATELY 35 COOKIES

These cookies taste like Panforte di Siena, a medieval dried fruit and nut confection. When the citrus in the Chiaraviglio garden is ripe to harvest, we begin the long process of candying lemon, grapefruit and orange peel to use throughout the year. The juice goes into making granita, semifreddo *or refreshing* spremuta.

300 g / 2 cups + 2 tbsp
all-purpose flour

4 g / 1 tsp baking powder

3 large eggs

2 g / 1 tsp ground cinnamon

2 g / 1 tsp finely ground
black pepper

1 g / ½ tsp ground cloves

Pinch of salt

350 g / 1¾ cups granulated sugar

350 g / 1¼ cups finely chopped
raw almonds

125 g / 2 cups
semisweet chocolate, grated

75 g / ⅓ cup
candied lemon peel, finely chopped

Grated zest of 1 lemon

Melted chocolate or confectioners'
sugar for topping (optional)

Sift the flour with the baking powder, salt and spices in a medium-size mixing bowl. Beat the eggs and sugar at high speed until white and fluffy. Add the dry ingredients, almonds, chocolate, candied orange and lemon peels and lemon zest. Mix until well combined. Wrap the dough first in parchment paper, then plastic film and refrigerate for 30 minutes. At this point the dough can be stored in the freezer for up to 2 months; defrost it before using.

To bake, preheat the oven to 160ºC / 325ºF.

Lightly dust your work surface with flour and roll out the dough to an even .5 cm / ¼ inch thickness. Cut the dough using a cookie cutter of your choice, re-roll the scraps and repeat. Transfer the cookies to cookie sheets lined with parchment paper, leaving 3 cm / 1 inch between each cookie.

Bake for 10–12 minutes.

These cookies can be finished with a drizzle of melted chocolate or a dusting of confectioners' sugar.

PANCIALE LIMA
FRUITCAKE BARS LIMA

***

YIELDS 35 COOKIES

Alessandro Lima, AAR's excellent barman, brought in this traditional Roman treat for the kitchen staff and we couldn't stop eating it. Ancient versions of panciale *or pan-giallo were baked with honey, dried fruit and nuts and brushed with egg yolk to resemble the sun and celebrate the Winter solstice. We make Panciale Lima in individual sizes for the AAR community.*

75 g / ½ cup + 1 tsp all-purpose flour	Preheat the oven to 150ºC / 300ºF.
250 g / 9 oz walnuts	Sift the flour to remove any lumps and combine with the walnuts, almonds, hazelnuts and chocolate. Warm this mixture in a double boiler until the chocolate begins to melt and then stir in the pine nuts and raisins, then finally the honey. Mix very well.
250 g / 9 oz almonds	
250 g / 9 oz hazelnuts	
250 g / 9 oz bittersweet chocolate, coarsely chopped	
125 g / 4½ oz pine nuts	Transfer the mixture onto a clean work surface and shape, using wet hands, into individual loafs 6 cm / 2½ inches x 2.5 cm / 1 inch.
c125 g / 4½ oz raisins	Bake for 10 minutes.
75 ml / 5 tbsp honey	Store up to 1 week in a sealed container.

MERINGHE

MERINGUE COOKIES

YIELDS 35-40 COOKIES

Kitty Travers, a visiting pastry chef from London, kindly taught Mirella how to make meringues. In the summer months we break meringues into a bowl and top them with fior di latte *gelato and macerated berries or poached apricots.*

8 egg whites

1 g / ¼ tsp salt

500 g / 2½ cups granulated sugar

Additional granulated sugar for dusting cookie sheets

Preheat the oven to 110°C / 225°F.

Beat the egg whites and salt at medium speed until they form soft peaks. Increase the speed of the mixer and add the sugar in a slow, steady stream until the meringue forms stiff glossy peaks.

Transfer the batter to a pastry bag and pipe spiral shapes of your choosing, approximately 2.5 cm / 1 inch in diameter, onto cookie sheets lined with parchment paper that has been dusted with granulated sugar.

Bake for 1 hour and 15 minutes until the cookies are very dry and firm. Turn off the heat and let the meringues continue to dry in the oven for another 30 minutes.

MERINGHE AL CACAO
CHOCOLATE MERINGUE COOKIES

YIELDS 35-40 COOKIES

This recipe is a variation of our standard meringue and is perfect for a brindisi *celebrating a staff birthday or a new baby.*

500 g / 2½ cups granulated sugar	Preheat the oven to 110ºC / 225ºF.
28 g / 4 tbsp cocoa powder	Combine the granulated sugar and cocoa powder.
8 egg whites	
1 g / ¼ tsp salt	Beat the egg whites and salt at medium speed until they form soft peaks. Increase the speed of the mixer and add the sugar-cocoa mix in a slow, steady stream until the meringue forms stiff glossy peaks.
Additional granulated sugar for dusting cookie sheets	
65 g / ½ cup bittersweet chocolate, melted	Transfer the batter to a pastry bag and pipe spiral shapes of your choosing, approximately 2.5 cm / 1 inch in diameter, onto cookie sheets lined with parchment paper that has been dusted with granulated sugar.

Bake for 1 hour and 15 minutes until the cookies are very dry and firm. Turn off the heat and let the meringues continue to dry in the oven for another 30 minutes.

Once cooled, gently dip the bottoms of the meringues into melted bittersweet chocolate.

These meringues keep well for up to 1 week in a sealed container.

MERINGHE AL CAFFÈ
COFFEE MERINGUE COOKIES

YIELDS 35-40 COOKIES

This is another meringue variation. In our meringhe al caffè we use finely ground pure Arabica espresso, which adds another dimension to this classic recipe.

10 g / 2 tbsp
finely ground espresso

8 egg whites

1 g / ¼ tsp salt

500 g / 2½ cups granulated sugar

Cocoa powder, for dusting

Preheat the oven to 110ºC / 225ºF.

Combine the sugar and ground espresso.

Beat the egg whites and salt at medium speed until they form soft peaks. Increase the speed of the mixer and add the sugar and ground espresso in a slow, steady stream until the meringue forms stiff glossy peaks.

Transfer the batter to a pastry bag and pipe spiral shapes of your choosing, approximately 2.5 cm / 1 inch in diameter, onto cookie sheets lined with parchment paper that has been dusted with granulated sugar.

Bake for 1 hour and 15 minutes until the cookies are very dry and firm. Turn off the heat and let the meringues continue to dry in the oven for another 30 minutes.

Once cool, dust with cocoa powder.

These meringues keep well for up to 2 weeks in a sealed container.

MERINGHE AL LIMONE E MANDORLE

MERINGUES WITH LEMON AND ALMONDS

YIELDS 35 COOKIES

The RSFP kitchen usually has leftover egg whites on hand, and this is a great way of using them up. Meringue cookies are especially great in summer when you crave something sweet but not rich to accompany your afternoon tea or coffee.

30 g / ¼ cup finely ground almonds, lightly toasted	Preheat the oven to 130ºC / 250ºF.

30 g / ¼ cup finely ground almonds, lightly toasted

2 egg whites

Salt

100 g / ½ cup superfine sugar

5 ml / 1 tsp fresh lemon juice

15 g / 1 tbsp cornstarch

15 g / ½ oz sliced almonds for topping

10g / 1 tbsp confectioners' sugar for dusting

Preheat the oven to 130ºC / 250ºF.

Pulse the almonds in a food processor until finely ground, but not yet a paste. Spread on a cookie sheet and toast in the oven for 10 minutes, or until just beginning to turn golden. Allow to cool before using.

Whip the egg whites and a pinch of salt at medium speed until frothy peaks form. Increase the speed and add the sugar in a steady stream and the lemon juice until the mixture forms stiff shiny peaks.

Combine the ground almonds and cornstarch in a small bowl and fold into the egg whites.

Transfer the meringue to a large pastry bag with a star tip. Pipe the meringue onto cookie sheets lined with parchment paper forming small 5-cm / 2-inch rings.

Top the meringues with sliced almonds and sprinkle with sifted confectioners' sugar.

Bake for 50–60 minutes, or until the meringues feel dry. Turn off the oven, open the door a crack and let the meringues continue to dry for another 30 minutes.

The cookies keep for up to 1 week in a container.

BISCOTTI AL CACAO E DULCE DI LATTE
COCOA COOKIES WITH CARAMELIZED MILK

Chocolate cookies are very good on their own, but sometimes when a dinner requires a more decadent dessert, we sandwich them with dulce di latte made with our delicious raw milk.

420 g / 3 cups all-purpose flour

105 g / 1 cup cocoa powder, sifted

1 g / ¼ tsp salt

10 g / 2½ tsp baking powder

225 g / 1 cup + 1 tbsp butter

250 g / 1¼ cups granulated sugar

2½ ml / ½ tsp vanilla extract

1 egg plus 1 yolk

Dulce di latte, optional

Sift the flour with the cocoa powder, salt and baking powder in a medium-size mixing bowl.

Cream the butter and sugar until light and fluffy. Add the vanilla extract and eggs and mix until well combined. Gradually add the dry ingredients and slowly mix until the dough comes together. Wrap the dough in plastic film and refrigerate for 30 minutes.

Transfer the dough to a lightly floured work surface. Divide the dough in two and shape each portion into logs 5 cm / 2 inches in diameter, taking care to not incorporate too much flour. At this point the cookies can be frozen for up to 2 months wrapped in a layer of parchment paper and plastic film.

To bake, preheat the oven to 180°C / 350°F.

Slice the logs into 5-mm / ¼-inch slices. Evenly space the cookies on cookie sheets lined with parchment paper, leaving 2 cm / ¾ inch between each cookie. Allow the dough to come to room temperature before baking.

Bake for 7–8 minutes.

If you spread the cookies with dulce di latte, they are best eaten the same day.

BISCOTTI AL CIOCCOLATO E CAFFÈ
CHOCOLATE AND COFFEE COOKIES

YIELD TEXT

These cookies are intense and flavorful. They go well with a caffè macchiato for an afternoon treat or with tangy blood orange granita for dessert.

100 g / ⅔ cup all-purpose flour

2 g / ½ tsp baking powder

Pinch of salt

350 g / 12 oz bittersweet chocolate, finely chopped

125 g / 4½ oz butter, cut into small pieces

3 large eggs

200 g / 1 cup granulated sugar

30 ml / 2 tbsp espresso or strong coffee

150 g / 5½ oz raw walnuts, roughly chopped

150 g / 5½ oz raw hazelnuts, roughly chopped

180 g / 6½ oz bittersweet chocolate, coarsely chopped

Preheat the oven to 180ºC / 350ºF.

Sift the flour, baking powder and salt in a medium-size mixing bowl.

Melt the finely chopped chocolate with the butter in a metal mixing bowl over lightly simmering water. Remove the bowl from the heat once the chocolate has completely melted and stir well.

Beat the egg, the yolk and sugar for 2 minutes at high speed until thick and light in color. Then add the melted chocolate-butter mixture and the espresso and mix slowly until well combined. By hand, fold in the nuts and chocolate pieces, and finally the dry ingredients.

Use a teaspoon to drop 16-g / ½-oz mounds of the dough onto cookie sheets lined with parchment paper, leaving 6 cm / 2½ inches between each cookie.

Bake for 15 minutes until the tops begin to crackle.

These cookies are best eaten freshly baked.

BISCOTTI AL CIOCCOLATA E ARANCIA

CHOCOLATE AND ORANGE COOKIES

———

YIELDS APPROXIMATELY 50 COOKIES

This recipe is a variation on our reliable chocolate wafer cookies and utilizes our bountiful supply of candied orange peel. Chocolate and orange make a fantastic combination. Sometimes we substitute candied pink grapefruit peel if we have some to use up.

420 g / 3 cups all-purpose flour

105 g / 1 cup cocoa powder, sifted

1 g / ¼ tsp salt

10 g / 2½ tsp baking powder

225 g / 1 cup + 2 tsp butter

250 g / 1¼ cup granulated sugar

Grated zest of 1 blood orange

1 egg plus 1 yolk

90 g / ½ cup candied blood orange peel, finely chopped

Sift the flour, cocoa powder, salt and baking powder in a medium-size mixing bowl.

Cream the butter, sugar and orange zest until light and fluffy. Add the egg and yolk and mix well. Gradually add the flour mixture and the peel, mix at low speed until well combined. Wrap the dough in plastic film and refrigerate for 30 minutes.

Transfer to a lightly floured work surface. Shape the dough into two logs 5 cm / 1½ inches in diameter, taking care not to incorporate too much flour. The logs can be frozen for up to 2 months wrapped in parchment paper and plastic film.

To bake, preheat the oven to 180°C / 350°F.

Slice the logs into 5-mm / ¼-inch-thick slices. Evenly space them on cookie sheets lined with parchment paper, leaving 2 cm / ¾ inch between each cookie. Allow the dough to come to room temperature before baking 7−8 minutes.

If you want to make these cookies really special, drizzle them with melted chocolate and garnish with more finely chopped candied peel.

They are best eaten freshly baked, but will keep in a container for 2−3 days.

BISCOTTI AL CIOCCOLATO E NOCCIOLE

CHOCOLATE HAZELNUT COOKIES

These rich chocolate hazelnut cookies are irresistible. One or two nights a year we serve them warm from the oven with cold milk for dessert at a Friday family dinner.

225 g / 8 oz hazelnuts, toasted, skinned and coarsely chopped

113 g / ½ cup + 1 tsp butter

90 g / ½ cup + 1 tbsp brown sugar

85 g / ⅓ cup + 5 tsp granulated sugar

2½ ml / ½ tsp vanilla extract

Pinch of salt

1 egg

180 g / 1⅓ cups all-purpose flour

3 g / ½ tsp baking soda

210 g / 7½ oz bittersweet chocolate, coarsely chopped

Cream the butter with the brown and granulated sugars until light and fluffy. Add the vanilla extract, salt and egg and continue to mix until well incorporated.

Whisk together the flour and baking soda in a medium-size mixing bowl. Add the dry mixture to the creamed butter and sugar. Add the nuts and chocolate and pulse the mixer until the dough comes together. Wrap the dough in plastic film and refrigerate for 30 minutes.

On a lightly floured surface, divide the dough in two and form each portion into logs 4 cm / 1½ inches in diameter. Wrap the logs first in parchment paper, then plastic film and freeze for 1 hour or up to 2 months.

To bake, preheat the oven to 180ºC / 350ºF.

Slice each log into thin slices approximately .5 cm / ¼ inch thick. Evenly space the cookies on cookie sheets lined with parchment paper, leaving 3 cm / 1½ inches between each cookie. Allow the dough to come to room temperature before baking. Bake for 10−12 minutes.

These cookies will keep for 2−3 days in a sealed container.

BIONDI DI BEN
BEN'S BLONDIES

———

YIELDS 32 COOKIES

Ben Barron lives in Rome with his family and volunteers in the Academy kitchen most Fridays after school. He is a naturally gifted pastry cook and is a pleasure to be around. These blondies are truly an indulgence—we cut them small to ease our guilt.

108 g / 8 tbsp butter, melted

80 g / ½ cup brown sugar

67 g / ⅓ cup granulated sugar

1 large egg

5 ml / 1 tsp vanilla extract

140 g / 1 cup all-purpose flour

6 g / 1 tsp salt

133 g / 1 cup bittersweet chocolate, coarsely chopped

115 g / 1 cup walnuts, coarsely chopped

Preheat the oven to 180°C / 350°F.

Cream the butter and two sugars at high speed until light and fluffy. Reduce the speed to low and pour in the egg and vanilla. Add the flour and salt and mix until just incorporated. Gently fold in half of the coarsely chopped chocolate and walnuts.

Prepare an 8-inch square baking pan by brushing it with butter, lining it with parchment paper and brushing the top of the paper with butter.

Transfer the batter to the prepared pan and sprinkle the top with the remaining chocolate and walnuts.

Bake for 35–40 minutes, until the top is golden brown and a toothpick inserted into the middle comes out clean. Once cooled, remove from the pan and slice into 32 bars.

These blondies are best eaten freshly baked.

ABOUT THE INGREDIENTS

The key to baking delicious tasting biscotti is using the best fresh ingredients from trusted sources.

Butter and milk: In the *Biscotti* cookbook, we use unsalted sweet cream butter with 82½% butter fat, which stays fresh if kept refrigerated at 1–6°C / 32–40°F for up to three months. When starting a recipe with butter remove it from the refrigerator and allow it to come to room temperature before proceeding with the creaming. All biscotti recipes use whole milk.

Chocolate and cocoa powder: The chocolate in the *Biscotti* cookbook is bittersweet and provides the requisite chocolaty flavor to the cookies. Chocolate must be stored in a cool, dry, dark place away from a heat source to prevent the cocoa fat from blooming (a white film that coats the chocolate) that can also change the texture of the chocolate from smooth and creamy to a less desirable crumbly. We use natural dark unsweetened cocoa powder in the *Biscotti* cookbook recipes.

Dried fruits, coconut and citrus: Taste dried raisins, figs and dates before purchasing; they should have concentrated bright flavor and a smooth texture. If they taste musty or the texture is grainy the dried fruit has been improperly dried or stored. Citrus skin should be shiny, clean and dry before zesting. In the *Biscotti* cookbook we use unsweetened shredded raw organic coconut. At the AAR we have tons of orange, lemon and grapefruit trees and we like to make our own candied peel, which is not difficult to do; however, one can fine delicious candied peel in small quantities in specialty stores.

Eggs: The eggs we use in our kitchen are large and organic. Egg whites are stored in a sealed container for up to two weeks in the refrigerator. Take eggs and egg whites out of the refrigerator and allow them to come to room temperature before making cookies or meringues. One large egg weighs 50 g / 1¾ oz, one egg yolk 30 g / ¾ oz, and one egg white 18 g / ⅕ oz.

Flour: Flour in Italy is graded differently from that in the United States. At the AAR we use several different types of flour for pasta and pastries. The majority of the recipes in the *Biscotti* book use *grano tenero tipo 0*, a soft summer wheat finely ground with 9–10% gluten. All-purpose flour is 9–12% gluten and a good equivalent. *Farina di farro*, farro flour, is becoming more common in Europe and North America as the demand for more nutritious flours increase and like *farina integrale*, whole wheat flour, it contains the whole grain and has a shorter shelf life. Cornmeal is equally susceptible to spoilage and is best bought in small quantities. All flours and grains need to be stored in a cool, dark and dry place in tightly sealed containers. If you do not plan on using the flour within a month, store it in the refrigerator to prevent the naturally present oils from turning rancid.

Honey: In the *Biscotti* cookbook we used *miele millefiori*, a golden un-pasteurized honey harvested each spring on a dairy farm just outside of Rome. A mild wildflower or clover honey is a good substitute. Raw honey can crystallize a few months after harvest and can be re-liquefied by placing the honey jar in hot water.

Jam: The American Academy in Rome has many fruit trees and when the fruit is at its peak in the Bass Garden we make *marmellata* to use throughout the year. Small batches of jam are easy to make but one can also purchase excellent quality jam that is not too sweet and is the essence of the fruit.

Olive oil and alcohol: At the AAR we use extra virgin cold pressed olive oil from Sabina, which mellows in flavor throughout the year. It also makes sense to use local wines in our Roman cookies and our homemade *nocino*.

Nuts and seeds: Almonds, hazelnuts, peanuts, pine nuts, pistachios, sesame seeds and walnuts are delicious, nutritious and often the most expensive baking ingredients. If possible, taste nuts and seeds before purchasing—if they taste oily or bitter, they aren't fresh and shouldn't be purchased. Buy whole raw nuts and seeds and toast and chop them yourself whenever possible. The exception to this is slivered or sliced almonds, which are processed with a machine and very difficult to cut evenly by hand.

We have found that it is best to toast nuts slowly at a low temperature (140°C / 285°F), which allows the nuts to cook more evenly, typically for 8–12 minutes. Sample a nut after 5 minutes to chart progress, redistribute the nuts on the cookie sheet and return to them to the oven to finish toasting to desired doneness.

After toasting hazelnut or walnuts, wrap them in clean dishtowel and rub vigorously to loosen the skins, which can be very bitter, transfer the nuts to a strainer and sift out the loose skins.

In the *Biscotti* cookbook we often grind/pulse raw nuts with small amounts of the measured sugar in a food processor so that the oil in the nuts combines with the sugar. This is how to avoid ending up with nut butters.

Raw nuts and seeds have delicate oils, which can very easily turn rancid if exposed to heat or sunlight. Nuts will absorb strong flavors if they are not stored in a sealed container. If the shelled nuts or seeds will be used within a month, store them in them in a dark cool cupboard or refrigerator, but for longer periods of time, they should be stored in the freezer, always labeled and dated.

Spices and salt: It is important to keep your spices fresh, old spices have a dull taste. Purchase small quantities and store spices away from a heat and light source. It is ideal to buy whole spices and grind them in small batches in a small electric coffee grinder, reserved for spices, for maximum flavor and perfume. We use *sale fino*, finely ground sea salt, in all the recipes where salt is added.

Sugar: At the RSFP we use organic unbleached granulated cane sugars. Demerara sugar is a coarsely granulated brown sugar, and has a mild molasses flavor. Dark brown sugar is moist and soft with a distinct molasses flavor. Confectioners sugar is a very fine cane sugar that has been mixed with cornstarch to prevent caking. Unsulphured molasses, a byproduct of sugar refining, is dark and strongly flavored.

Vanilla: Vanilla is expensive and good quality vanilla extract is hard to find in Italy. At the AAR we make our own by steeping 7–8 Madagascar vanilla beans cut open and scraped into 750 ml / 25 oz light rum, allowing the flavor to mature for 2–3 months in a cool dark place. We also save any used vanilla bean pods. Rinse the vanilla beans, let them air dry for 24 hours then bury them in confectioners sugar or granulated sugar to use in other baking projects that require a vanilla flavor.

TECHNIQUES, METHODS
AND EQUIPMENT

It is true that even the best-written and clearest recipes are only guidelines; it is the cook's instinct, practical experience and common sense that will make a recipe succeed. While these recipes were mainly conceived, written and tested in a professional kitchen in Rome, we believe that they translate well into a home kitchen.

Before starting a new *biscotti* recipe, read it over carefully, gather your ingredients and equipment and take your time; don't rush. We have found that it takes a beginning cook three times to really understand and perfect a new recipe.

I encourage you to make notes in the margin of the recipes, including the date the recipe was made and any observations or possible substitutions of ingredients. I find this makes baking personal and the recipe more familiar when you make it again.

To scale up a recipe for an institution one needs to simply multiply the ingredients for the desired yield. It is best to do batches of the recipe no more than 5 times. Mixing times may take longer to achieve the desire consistency. Weighing ingredients is the most efficient way to achieve excellent results. It is also the simplest way to teach baking and is essential in controlling food costs. Electronic scales are ideal for professional baking. Scaling a recipe up or down is best done in gram measurement; all good professional kitchens convert to metric measurement for production baking.

In the AAR kitchen Mirella regularly makes biscotti dough a day ahead and let it "rest" before rolling out the individual balls or logs. This resting period allows the ingredients come together, chill and relax...very Italian. It also makes sense when doing production baking, devoting a day to making mixes and then another day to rolling logs and balls. The cookie balls are transferred to a sealed container and logs are double wrapped, everything is carefully labeled and stored in the freezer for later use.

In the RSFP kitchen we use professional equipment and supplies. We are dependent on our 1-litre electric mixer and a 20-litre freestanding mixer for large batches and our food processor for grinding nuts, however, these recipes can be made by hand. A mixer and food processor are good investments if you are going to make cookies on a regular basis.

We use parchment paper for baking and wrapping cookie dough. This prevents cookies from sticking to cookie sheets, eases the clean up and preserves the life of the cookie sheets.

Label a cutting board, wooden spoons, rolling pins, rubber spatulas "pastry only" as you do not want to transfer unwanted flavors to your cookies. A good pair of thick oven mitts is essential—grabbing a dishtowel to remove hot trays from the oven often leads to burns. Investing in good cookie cutters is worth it. Wipe them dry after each use, and if they need to be washed, dry them in a very low oven to prevent rust.

Pastry cooks are notorious for having dull knives, which can be dangerous, as you will need to use more pressure to cut nuts, chocolate or citrus peel which can cause you to slip and cut yourself. Keeping your knives sharp is important, and makes the work easier and prevents injuries.

Trust yourself, and watch the oven closely. The temperatures and times we have listed for biscotti recipes are what work best for us. If you see that your cookies are getting too brown too quickly, turn down the temperature by a few degrees. If the cookies are still too soft when the time is up, leave them in a couple of more minutes and take note. Ovens thermometers are notoriously finicky and often calibrated incorrectly. Many cooks rotate their cookies in the oven half way through cooking, if you see that the cookies are baking unevenly, go ahead and do this. We haven't listed this as a step in the *Biscotti* book, since we rarely need to do so.

INDEX

ACKNOWLEDGEMENTS

Mona Talbott and Mirella Misenti are extremely grateful to Francesca Gilberti RSFP intern 2007, 2008, 2009, 2010 and April Word, RSFP intern 2010, who were essential in the early and final stages of translating, testing, and standardizing recipes, and to our beloved colleagues Christopher Boswell, Domenico Cortese, Alessandro Lima, Gabriel Soare and Tsige Tekka.

Mirella Misenti dedicates the book to her family for their unwavering support and in particular to her children Piero and Lorena.

Mona Talbott dedicates this first RSFP cookbook to Prof. Carmela Vircillo Franklin, AAR Director 2005 to 2009, whose discerning taste and wisdom has guided the RSFP in a myriad of ways.

The success of the Rome Sustainable Food Project is due in large part to our extraordinary interns without whom the food project could not exist; they are hard-working, dedicated cooks and the driving spirit behind all the food that comes out of the AAR kitchen. Special thanks to Benjamin Barron, Peter Beck, Brian Bligh, Lisa Costa, Katrina Grandage, Camilla Houstoun, Kitty Travers and Mary Pat Walsh.

A big thank you to the current and former Fellows, Staff and the entire AAR community for eating and enjoying the RSFP biscotti!

Last and most important, thank you to the very talented and patient Annie Schlechter whose photos and design bring this book to life.

BISCOTTI

A NOTE ON THE TITLING TYPE

The Italian cookie names are set in Saturn, a typeface based on the inscription on the Temple of Saturn in the Roman Forum. The word BISCOTTI on the cover and title page is based on a jewelry shop sign in Lucca, Italy. Both were designed by Russell Maret, a type designer and letterpress printer who was the Rolland Rome Prize Fellow in Design at the American Academy in Rome 2010.

A B C D E F G H I J K L M N O P Q R S T U V W X Y Z

AMERICAN ACADEMY IN ROME

The American Academy in Rome is a center for independent study and advanced research in the arts and humanities. For more than 116 years the Academy has offered support, time and an inspiring environment to some of America's most gifted artists and scholars. Each year, through a national juried competition, the Academy offers up to thirty Rome Prize fellowships in architecture, design, historic preservation and conservation, landscape architecture, literature, musical composition, visual arts, and in humanistic approaches to ancient studies, medieval studies, Renaissance and early modern studies, and modern Italian studies. Fellows are joined by a select group of Residents, distinguished artists and scholars invited by the Director. Many Academy Fellows and Residents have had a significant influence in the worlds of art, music, culture, literature, scholarship and education.

Founded in 1894, the Academy was chartered as a private institution by an act of Congress in 1905. The Academy remains a private institution supported by gifts from individuals, foundations and corporations, and the membership of colleges, universities and arts and cultural organizations, as well as by grants from the National Endowment for the Arts, the National Endowment for the Humanities and the United States Department of Education.

www.aarome.org

THE ROME SUSTAINABLE FOOD PROJECT

The Rome Sustainable Food Project, a program devoted to providing organic, local and sustainable meals for the community of the American Academy in Rome, has launched a delicious revolution to rethink institutional dining. Headed by chef Mona Talbott, a Chez Panisse alum, and guided by Alice Waters, the menus have given rise to a new, authentic cuisine, inspired by *la cucina romana*, Chez Panisse, and the collective experience of those working in the AAR kitchen. A logical extension of the Academy's values, since its official launch in February 2007, the Rome Sustainable Food Project has transformed the community of the American Academy in Rome with a collaborative dining program that nourishes and supports both work and conviviality and aims to construct a replicable model for sustainable dining in an institution.

Carmela Vircillo Franklin, Director of the American Academy in Rome from 2005 to 2010, writes:

Every weekday at 4:30 pm, tea is served in the salone of the American Academy in Rome. The table is set and then right on the dot, Alessandro Lima, a member of the kitchen staff, wheels in steaming pots of tea, along with a tray of delicious but simple biscotti baked by Mirella Misenti. Those who gather in the salone for tea represent the Academy community at large: Fellows, Residents and their families; staff members; visiting artists and scholars; Library readers; and other guests.

Conversation and the exchange of ideas across fields and disciplines among our large and diverse community are central to the mission of the Academy, and it is around such events as afternoon tea that the poet is given an opportunity to talk with the archeologist, the visiting architect learns about the project of the Rome prize winner in Historic Preservation, Roman readers of our Library discuss comparative political systems with our Fellows. Afternoon tea, which nourishes both body and mind, contributes gracefully and appreciably to these goals.

ABOUT THE AUTHORS

Mona Talbott was chosen by Alice Waters to be the Executive Chef of the Rome Sustainable Food Project in 2006. The RSFP officially launched February 26, 2007, to establish a sustainable eco-gastronomic cuisine authentic to the American Academy in Rome. Talbott is a mentor to many cooks starting their careers and is a respected teacher, author and chef.

Her first food-related job was working in large reforestation camps in Canada. After culinary school she was hired by Alice Waters to work at Chez Panisse. She later worked at Eli Zabar's Vinegar Factory and E.A.T. stores in New York and consulted for Hillary Clinton at her home in Chappaqua, New York. In 1999, Talbott began working as a chef for photographer Annie Leibovitz, and in 2004, was hired by Bette Midler's New York Restoration Project to design a children's after-school gardening and cooking program. In 2009, she was selected to be in *COCO: 10 World-leading Masters Choose 100 Contemporary Chefs*. She has written articles and recipes for *The New York Times*, *Saveur* and *Organic Style*.

Mirella Misenti is the pastry cook at the American Academy in Rome. Born in Melilli, Sicily, a small town outside of Siracusa, she has had a lifelong passion for traditional Sicilian pastries. In 2007 Mirella joined the Rome Sustainable Food Project cooks, bringing with her a knowledge of *dolce Italiano*, which helped to define the cuisine at the American Academy in Rome.

ABOUT THE PHOTOGRAPHERS

Annie Schlechter has been working as a photographer since 1998. She spent from September 2009 to June 2010 living at the American Academy in Rome. Her clients include *The World of Interiors*, *House Beautiful*, *The New York Times Magazine*, *Real Simple*, *W* magazine, *Travel & Leisure*, and many more.

Matthew Monteith earned an MFA from the Yale School of Art. He has been a Fulbright Scholar and a fellow at the American Academy in Rome. He lives in New York City.